Protecting Your Collection

*A Handbook, Survey, & Guide
for the Security of Rare Books,
Manuscripts, Archives, & Works of Art*

About the Author

Slade Richard Gandert is a Pintard Fellow of The New York Historical Society, a member of the Association of Former Intelligence Officers, and a member of the American Society for Industrial Security. He holds several post graduate degrees and has served as a consultant for SRI International.

His latest venture is the operation of the Fine Arts Protection Consortium, Ltd. of which he is the founder. This international firm specializes in museum and library theft prevention and security with particular emphasis on rare book and manuscript theft. Mr. Gandert still maintains an interest in The Literary Lions, a business research consulting firm he founded several years ago.

An avid sportsman, he also collects books on subjects ranging from field sports to Robert Frost. He divides his time between New York and New Hampshire. Mr. Gandert is currently at work on an espionage novel and a work of non fiction.

Readers wishing to contact Mr. Gandert should address their correspondence to the Fine Arts Protection Consortium, Ltd., 127 East 59 Street, New York, NY 10022.

Protecting Your Collection

A Handbook, Survey, & Guide
for the Security of Rare Books,
Manuscripts, Archives, & Works of Art

Slade Richard Gandert, MS, MLS

Library & Archival Security
Volume 4, Numbers 1/2

The Haworth Press
New York

The Haworth Press, Inc., 28 East 22 Street, New York, NY 10010

Library of Congress Cataloging in Publication Data

Gandert, Slade Richard.
    Protecting your collection.

    (Library & archival security; v. 4, no. 1-2)
    Bibliography: p.
    1. Libraries—Special collections—Security measures—Handbooks, manuals, etc. 2. Archives—Security measures—Handbooks, manuals, etc. 3. Libraries, Rental—Security measures—Handbooks, manuals, etc. I. Title. II. Series.
Z679.6.L5 vol. 4, no. 1-2   025.8'2s   81-7004
ISBN 0-917724-78-X   [025.8'2]   AACR2

To my father, Philip Gandert, who taught me the values of honor, simplicity, and loyalty.

To my wife, Louise, who provided me with rigorous criticism rather than sycophancy.

Protecting Your Collection

Library & Archival Security
Volume 4, Numbers 1/2

FOREWORD

In the main, this book is not technical in nature. It illustrates accounts of sometimes sad, sometimes humorous, and nearly always unfortunate experiences of librarians across the nation who have lost valuable parts of their collections through thievery, fire, or flooding. Priceless collections are ravaged each year through criminal attack or disaster. Today's Library Administrators cannot afford to ignore these growing problems.

Library Security is a field in which the problems are as diverse as they are numerous. It is axiomatic that no single person can be an expert in every phase of security. The very nature of the security profession mitigates against theoretical solutions to real problems of security. *Protecting Your Collection* is must reading for Library Administrators and security practitioners as well. They will recognize that the author has done his homework. The methods and procedures illustrated in this text are from documented case histories.

In most cases, the losses outlined occurred as a result of a "weak-link" creating an area of vulnerability in the total security defense. The theft succeeded because the thief surveyed, studied, and researched his target's security defenses. Serious fire damage occurs as a result of a lack of early warning detection devices, carelessness, and an ignorance of basic fire safety precautions. Through this reading, it is hoped that the reader will benefit from the mistakes of others and learn how to more effectively increase security awareness.

It is timely that this book has been written when most Library Administrators are eagerly searching for effective solutions to the ever increasing problem of theft and disaster. This is not a theoretical nor a 'how to prevent' treatise. *Protecting Your Collection* is a practical text authored by a very respected librarian and security consultant who is well grounded in all aspects of library and museum security.

John Erickson, CPP
Superintendent of Security
New York Public Library System

PREFACE

Our great institutions are being plundered. The furtive snap of swag-filled attache cases reverberates throughout the land. Many of the specialists in these institutions believe that security concerns are either beneath their dignity or irrelevant since scholars do not steal. The rise of the scholar-thief belies such attitudes. What is even more invidious is misguided egalitarianism which is causing some to increase rather than decrease collection access.

Theft is a growth industry. The rise of "collectibles" as investments has made the public more aware of those items which were once the province of scholars. A crime in which there is negligible risk exposure and spectacular profits will not long remain the province of a select band of thieves.

Annual losses are equal to amounts equivalent to between 14 and 23 percent of acquisition budgets. When we speak of rare book and manuscript and other specialized collections the figures soar. It was reported that over 12,000 books, films and musical scores are lost through theft and vandalism at the Metro Toronto Library each year.

Thomas Hardy wrote: "If a way to the better there be, it exacts a full look at the worst." It is my intention to compel many to take that look.

Slade Richard Gandert
North Conway, New Hampshire

Acknowledgments

There are many persons whose anonymity must be maintained. Without their trust and cooperation there would have been lacunae in many chapters. To them I express my gratitude.

Special thanks are extended to Paul Rugen, Keeper of Manuscripts, Research Libraries of the New York Public Library; Robert Volpe, New York City Police Department Detective; Egon Weiss, Director of Libraries United States Military Academy, West Point; Frank De Rosa, Security Chief Brooklyn Public Library.

Thanks also are extended to Jesse Taub for his reading of the manuscript and his valuable recommendations. I would like to thank John Shaheen for his encouragement.

CREDITS

Keep your Books behind stout
Gratings, and in no wise let
any Person come at them to take
them from the Shelf except Yourself.

The Old Librarian's Almanack
by "Philobiblos" (Jared Bean)
New Haven, Conn. 1773

He who wants to present a corrective must know
thoroughly what the existing weaknesses are.

Soren Kierkegaard

THE SITUATION

The situation regarding library and museum security bears a resemblance to that of library and museum fire prevention measures of more than a century ago. Only a few people then seemed to realize that there was a fire risk, and yet there were those who inveighed against attitudes and precepts which categorically labeled buildings as fireproof. Warning the New York State Legislature about the fire risk to the New York State Library, the State Librarian, Melvil Dewey, wrote; "In our manuscript room are collections which have cost the state vast sums and which money could not replace, and yet there is no place to keep them except a room honeycombed with oak and interlaced with electric wires."[1]

Despite his eminence in the field of library science, Dewey's remarks were considered alarmist. Evidently the fact that the New York State Library was ensconced in the massive Capitol Building was enough to convince Dewey's critics that existing fire protection arrangements were adequate. The fire that overtook this library in November 1911 was saddeningly spectacular. The then fifth largest library in the nation, and one ranked in the first twenty of the world, was nearly destroyed. Albany residents watched the night sky aghast, as "flying sheets of scorched paper—historical manuscripts and pages out of books—flecked the sky over Albany like snowflakes."[2]

The occurrence of great library fires has not, in the opinion of some fire risk specialists, caused the library community to address itself suitably to the fire risk. John Morris believes that the fact that there has not been an incidence of fires sufficient to categorize libraries as bad fire risks has been at the heart of the problem.[3]

At the moment, many great collections remain at peril. Concluding his work *Managing the Library Fire Risk*, Morris poses the pivotal question: "Why is it that we can never find money to provide for adequate protection of our most priceless resources, but after disaster strikes we can always find money for rebuilding?"[4]

This question is one which we shall consider in reference to library and museum security. First, however, it is necessary to understand the difference between the areas of security and fire prevention. Both areas have been delegated, in many instances, to persons of little authority in their institutions and sometimes with little knowledge in such areas.

Security is a way of life. Caution and restraint characterize the actions of the security officer. And if at times he views the world with some suspiciousness—and even cynicism—it is simply because trustworthiness appears to be a commodity of which the world has never been in large supply.

Security officers can be expected to exhibit all the foibles and crotchets of other people; that is, they are normal members of society. In matters of security, however, zeal is the watchword. Richard Drain, a former CIA Director of Operations, is now engaged in fund raising in Washington, DC for the National Cathedral. Drain's colleagues were fascinated by his practice of turning his "in" and "out" baskets upside down. He did this, he informed them, to satisfy nonexistent security officers that no classified documents remained once he had left his desk.[5]

There are people who ignore even ordinary precepts of security. To many the very term *police* is pejorative. Consider the statement of Metropolitan Museum of Art Director Phillippe de Montebello, "I don't have to be a policeman for somebody else's tradition."[6] The security professional, who can be a former law enforcement officer, is frequently misunderstood by the academic world. Many people consider security to be merely and extension of the police function. This view, of course, colors their attitudes toward security and those engaged in its practice.

The public is aware that the police experience tends to shape a person to its needs. The police system brings about a change in its workers, so that even a normally mild person is transformed into the authoritarian personality which is required by the profession.[7]

There are, in fact, times when the security professional is

regarded as a tradesman who is trying to enter a resplendent residence by the front door. While trade is necessary, those entering for the purpose of trade are expected to use the tradesmen's entrance at the back.

An example of disregard for security recommendations found its way into the pages of the *New York Times*. William H. Honan, a *New York Times* writer researching material for a pair of articles, had wanted to see "the vault" at the Metropolitan Museum of Art. This is an area which is of vital concern to the security staff. Honan reported the following encounter with the museum's director, de Montebello:

> He shook his head and said that the museum's security department had vetoed my request. I pressed him on the matter, and suffice it to say Mr. de Montebello was soon prompting an assistant to override the security department and make the necessary arrangements to open the vault for us.[8]

It should be understood that effective security is founded on the "need to know" principle. That is to say, one only knows as much about security as is necessary for his or her function. Honan's admission to the vault was in violation of this time-proven system:

> He would take me on a brief inspection tour of this "holy of holies"... provided that I would give no hint as to its location in the museum nor describe the type of lock on its door. Also, no photographs would be allowed.[9]

Actually, by his "tour" Honan learned more about that area than may have been known by some security personnel. De Montebello's casualness illustrates the problem with which security interests find themselves doing constant battle. Everyone recognizes the need for security, but security precautions are often tossed aside lightly.

Belief as to what constitutes deterrent effect ranged from the otiose to the simplistic:

> At first the Met wasn't sure what to do with a tunnel thirty-two feet in diameter and nearly a quarter of a mile long. In

the early years it was used for well-publicized pistol practice by the guards—their high standard of marksmanship being considered a deterrent to art thieves.[10]

A further problem is evidenced in the article "Artful Thieves," which deals with the recovery of stolen art objects in the United States. The heroes are none other than agents if the revered Scotland Yard. The role of American law enforcement officials was, in this instance, relegated to praise of the Yard by the F.B.I.: Thomas M. McShane, as FBI special agent in New York City who specialized in art-theft cases, says, "There's no question that they're very good at their business: they're tops."[11] The implication is that American law enforcement officials merely sit in awe as Scotland Yard and other foreign agencies perform their miracles. The same article ends with a ringing denunciation of the lack of such a squad in New York City. Bonnie Burnham, Executive Director of the New York Foundation for Art Research, is quoted in the final sentence of the article: "The London art theft squad had made dealers sensitive to the problem—and that's part of their success. A group like this is something the art world in New York could relate to".[12]

There are vast differences in the manner in which British and American law enforcement establishments view art thefts. The minimum sentence for art theft in England is usually five years, while in America it is a rarity for a jail sentence to be given.[13] According to Detective Superintendent Thomas of Scotland Yard,

> After all when art is stolen part of the national heritage is stolen. Something which your children will want in the future, their sense of history is damaged. And if you refuse to identify any crime for what is is, whether it is housebreaking or whatever, it will only increase.[14]

A curious condition is noted in any discussion of art theft. Art thieves are accorded elite status and often are regarded by the public with awe and fascination. Keith Middlemas indicates that the fact that the average man can never possess items like those stolen, coupled with the notion that the thief is "a potential Raffles despoiling the privileged elite"[15] conspires to place public sympathy with the thief rather with the institution which suffers the loss. The romanticism attending ideas of the elegant thief, along with the lenient manner with which cases of art theft are handled by courts in the United States, complicates the security problems of museums and other public institutions.

It is an unfortunate fact the thievery is aided and abetted by the willingness of certain persons to purchase stolen goods. We are in the midst of the age of the collector. People want a hedge against inflation, and they sometimes turn to works of art to fill this need. It is here that the impact of the double market arises. The double market is made up of clandestine dealers and patrons who will purchase stolen art works. Often the recipient of a stolen work of art will keep the work for his or her own collection. There are others, dealers in the main, who undertake, at immense profit to themselves, to ship stolen works of art to other parts of the world. Middlemas writes; "The double market cannot be eradicated; immoral but inevitable, it is, in truth, as much a phenomena of our times as share watering and company fraud were of earlier brasher stages of industrial society."[16]

The various types of thieves, their motivations, and their successes and failures continue to be studied. The work and planning that are required in the carrying out of some thefts are as remarkable as the simplicity with which others are accomplished. The judicial system does not provide a meaningful deterrent to the art thief, as the intrinsic value of art items is generally not recognized by the court. The willingness of some collectors to buy what they know are stolen items and the growth of the number of thefts by academics are sobering comments on the moral tone of the age.

The men and women of the world of professional security who pit their skills against the onslaught of thieves, both professional and amateur, are constantly working against such odds. Yet the situation is not as bleak as may be imagined. Security matters are gradually being given the attention they deserve. If these are slighted in some quarters, it is nevertheless true that there is a growing understanding of their importance.

NOTES

1. Cecil R. Roseberry, *A History of the New York State Public Library*, p. 81.
    2. Ibid.

3. John Morris, *Managing the Library Fire Risk*, p. 3.
4. Ibid., p. 123.
5. Peter Wyden, *Bay of Pigs: The Untold Story*, p. 329.
6. William H. Honan, "The Once and Future Met," *New York Times*, July 8, 1979, p. 24.
7. Arthur Niederhoffer, *Behind the Shield: The Police in an Urban Society*, p. 118.
8. William H. Honan, "The Hidden Met," *New York Times Magazine*, July 1, 1979, p. 40.
9. Ibid., pp. 40-41.
10. Honan, "The Once and Future Met," p. 22.
11. Pranay Gupte, "Artful Thieves," *New York Times Magazine*, July 22, 1979, p. 58.
12. Ibid., p.62.
13. Laurie Adams, *Art Cop Robert Volpe: Art Crime Detective*, p. 12.
14. Det. Supt. Thomas, quoted in *Art Cop*, p. 12.
15. Keith Middlemas, *The Double Market: Art Theft and Art Thieves*, p. 19.
16. Ibid., p. 227.

*It is part of my creed that the only poetry
is history, could we tell it right.*

Thomas Carlyle

LIBRARY SECURITY: AN OVERVIEW

A barometer of the extent of library theft and mutilation is found in the treatment of these matters in literature. The attitude until comparatively recently was one bordering on indifference. Thefts were discounted; missing items were items that had been misplaced. Now, however, the existence of library crime is gradually being acknowledged, and steps are being instituted to combat it.

One of these steps is the publication of lists of missing items. The Society of American Archivists issues annually its *National Register of Lost or Stolen Archive Materials*, an item that is reprinted in *Library and Archival Security*. Furthermore, such publications as the *Library Journal* and the *Antiquarian Bookman* give extensive, if occasional, coverage to stories of thefts from libraries.

Library losses began to be reported in 1909. In that year, a one-page article entitled "Inventory: Report of the ALA Committee on Library Administration"[1] appeared in the *ALA Bulletin*. In May 1917, *Library Journal* devoted three pages to a discussion of a more complete inventory procedure in an article entitled "A New Kind of Inventory."[2] There was no mention of security measures in either article, although in both the problem of misplaced items was explored. The concern was at the time to simplify inventory procedures.

A Survey of Libraries in the United States, by the American Library Association, dealt with "Inventory, Insurance and Accounting in 1927.[3] It was still held that missing books were simply misplaced and that these could be found by instituting formidable inventory control procedures. The spectre which

7

would come to haunt manuscript librarians, insurance of the collection, was also mentioned. In 1927 also the *Library Journal* published a one-page article entitled "Frequency of Inventory."[4]

It was in August of 1935 that Ralph Munn of the Pittsburgh Public Library saw fit to write an article called "Problems of Theft and Mutilation." In this article the thesis was advanced that patrons occasionally steal and mutilate materials.[5]

Early in 1966 an article appeared, almost unnoticed, which was a portent of things to come. Ruth Anne Bean's "Theft and Mutilation of Books, Magazines, and Newspapers" appeared in the January-March 1936 issue of *Library Occurrent.*[6]

Three years later *The American Archivist* published Randolph G. Adams's "The Character and Extent of Fugitive Archival Materials."[7] This article contained a discussion of misplaced and lost items; no consideration was given to the theft problem.

One of the first major articles dealing with this problem appeared in the *New York Public Library Bulletin* of September 1944. This was Lawrence S. Thompson's "Notes on Biblioklepto-mania."[8] The term "bibliokleptomania," Thompson's own, has since then gained some currency in the language. Although Thompson highlighted a situation with which librarians were even then becoming all too familiar, his article elicited little response.

Eventually, however, the climate did change in the world of archives and manuscripts. Robert H. Land addressed the problem of manuscript theft in the April 1956 issue of the *American Archivist.* His article, "Defense of Archives Against Human Foes,"[9] included an evaluation of theft by staff members. Vigorous prosecution was suggested as a solution to this problem.

Little by little, the disappearance of rare books began to be reported. Regarded as a few scattered incidents, these were written off as serious but not indicative of a wave of such thefts. They were considered deeds of the misguided, rather than the work of professional thieves. Tangentially, the American Library Association became aware of what was occurring and began a technology project that was concerned with security measures. The resulting report, published in 1963, *Protecting the Library and Its Resources: A Guide to Physical Protection and Insurance,*[10] dealt with fire, floods, and other considerations. Little attention was given to the matter of theft.

Thefts, however, continued to take place, and the intrinsic trust of librarians for their public was slowly but markedly eroding. In April 1965, the *Library Journal* carried an article by John N. Berry that was boldly titled "To Catch a Thief."[11] Polite euphemisms were dropped, and a thief was called a thief.

Concern was mounting. The February 1966 issue of the *Library Journal* contained an article which asked the question: "Your Charging System: Is It Thiefproof?"[12] Authors Robert Clark and George Haydee challenged their audience to think about the theft problem. Again, although the article dealt with circulation, the problem of security was being addressed.

The nomenclature of the security professional was beginning to find its way into the administrator's vocabulary. The May 1967 issue of *College and Research Libraries* contained George Eiser's "Exit Controls and the Statewide Card."[13] The security problem was being seen in terms of manual security devices in the Summer 1968 issue of *Southeastern Librarian*. Here Ernst Weyhrauch and Mary Thurman commented upon the efficiency of such devices in "Turnstiles, Checkers and Library Security."[14]

Despite efforts to secure library collections, thefts continued at an alarming rate. The sociological approach to a cure to the problem was entertained in a Spring 1969 article in *School Libraries*. This was Roman Vinnes' "Search for Meaning in Book Thefts."[15] Then, in 1970, Maxine H. Reneker's "Study of Book Thefts in Academic Libraries" was accepted by the University of Chicago as his master's thesis.[16]

In that same year the American Library Association issued a *Library Technology Report* called a *Survey of Theft Detection Systems*.[17] With this report the security problem attained more visibility than it had ever had previously. A few years later, in 1973, the Burns Security Institute published its *National Survey of Library Security*.[18] And in the following year, another "Library Technology Report," *Theft Detection Systems for Libraries: A Survey*, appeared. This was an updated version of the 1970 report.

A significant event in the field of manuscript and library security was the appearance in 1975 of the *Library Security Newsletter*. The premier issue contained an article by Lawrence S. Thompson of the University of Kentucky entitled "New Reflections on

Bibliokleptomania."[20] In this article Thompson updated the views he had presented in his original 1944 article in the *New York Public Library Bulletin*.

Manuscripts and archive materials in general were of great concern. Timothy Walch, of the Society of American Archivists, saw to it that the Society's *Newsletter* of July 1976 contained a segment entitled "Archival Security Newsletter."[21] Later in that year he began the publication of *Security Register*,[22] a list of lost and stolen manuscript items. These two efforts gave expression to the pressing need for manuscript security.

A 1976 doctoral dissertation entitled "A Survey of the Attitudes Toward and Utilization of Security Measures in Selected Academic Libraries" dealt with the Southeastern United States.[23] The focus of the study was the attitudes people brought to matters of security, rather than the institution of security programs. Security personnel were not contacted in the study made by the author, Donald Bruce Robinson, although a questionnaire was mailed to various libraries.

In 1977 Timothy Walch published *Archives and Manuscripts Security*.[24] This thirty-page handbook provides an incisive overview of the field. The author dealt with matters from door locks to detection devices. Also included was a security checklist. This work was the first of its kind, and its appearance was welcomed.

Also in 1977 the *AB Bookman's Weekly* responded to the alarming theft rate with a section entitled "Missing Books." The rationale for the section was as follows:

> This section, open to all—dealers, libraries and collectors—is for the rapid notification to the book trade throughout the world of the recent theft or loss of valuable books, manuscripts, maps, prints or other items that may subsequently be identified and possibly recovered. All items listed have been reported as missing as of press time of the week in which they appear.[25]

Among the entries in the first list, which appeared in the July 11-18 issue, by far the most striking was that of the Plymouth State College Library regarding books of Robert Frost which were missing:

Plymouth State College Library
Plymouth, NH 03264 (603) 536-1550 Ext 257
Att: Janice Gallinger, Director
Frost, R., Boy's Will, London, 1913;
Inscribed: "RF w/kind regards, May 10, 1951"
- Mountain Interval, first issue, 1916;
Inscribed: "Your always friendly Robert Frost"
RF autograph Corrections pp. 88 & 93 (?)
- New Hampshire, 1923, signed: "Yours always
Robert Frost" Webster bookplate
- North of Boston, 1915 reprint; Inscribed
"Your Friend RF of Franconia" Webster bookplate
- Witness Tree, 1942; Inscribed: "Yours always
Robert Frost".[26]

The college has many books which Frost gave to two friends. One of these, Ernest Silver, was a principal at the Plymouth Normal School, where Frost taught in 1911, a few years before he made the trip to England during which he published *A Boy's Will*.[27] The other friend, a man Frost met in 1915, was George H. Browne,[28] whose Frost collection is housed in one of the college's special collections.

In the following year, 1978, a highly technical and detailed work on security systems was published. This was Alice Harrison Bahr's *Book Theft and Library Security Systems: 1978-1979*.[29] In this work, which was published by Knowledge Industry Publications, evaluations were given of a variety of the systems then on the market. Details of operation areas were clearly defined.

Forbes Magazine, on April 16, 1979, ran an article entitled "The Game Where Nobody Loses but Everybody Loses,"[30] in which the theft epidemic was surveyed. Author Richard Phalon indicated that law enforcement officials believed that less than fifty percent of objects reported stolen were recovered. The further supposition was posited that reported thefts of manuscripts, rare books, and art objects were but a miniscule portion of the total number occurring.

The overall security problems at the New York Public Library were chronicled and commented upon by David Aikman in an article which appeared in the October 8, 1979 issue of *Time* magazine, entitled "In New York Reading Between the Lions."[31] The article, which quoted security personnel at the New York Public Library, described the lawlessness of certain patrons and the lack of trained guards.

An indication of how library offenses have caught the public attention is found in the *New York Times Book Review* of October 14, 1979.[32] This issue contained a reproduction of a cartoon from the book *Nuts* by Graham Wilson showing the contents of a boy's solvenly bureau drawer. Among the items was a "library book too overdue to take back."[33]

A few weeks later the *Book Review* contained a review of the fiction work *Provenance*, by Frank McDonald. The novel deals with international art theft. An indication of the subject matter can be gained from the review: "Mr. McDonald is an author who does not waste precious research; there are little lectures on are forgeries and the latest methods of detection."[34] The book, which has been the subject of full-page advertisements and is to be made into a movie, was one of the first with a plot concerning art theft. This particular crime has evidently come of age.

Rare book and manuscript thefts also received attention in this same *Book Review*. In the "Crime" column of "Newgate Callendar" (a humorous pseudonym), a review appeared of Lawrence Bloch's mystery novel, *The Burglar Who Liked to Quote Kipling.* This novel tells the story of one Bernie Rhodenbarr, who is hired "to steal a rare book from a rich collector."[35]

Books such as this tend to bring the prevalence of library thefts into public view. Whether or not this has value is a question to which there is no easy answer. Robert Schnare, Special Collections Librarian at the U.S. Military Academy at West Point, speaks of the recent rash of thefts involving Winslow Homer lithographs: "It's like a two edged sword; if you don't publicize it nobody knows about it, but if you publicize it then someone realizes the Winslow Homers are worth something. Boom! Amateur people start ripping them off."[36]

Actually, librarian archivists no longer have a choice. Theft of books and manuscripts has now reached alarming proportions, and security specialists are now found on the staffs of almost all sizable libraries and archival institutions. It may not be entirely fanciful to suggest that a new hero is arriving on the scene, the dashing, young investigator who, like McDonald's hero, Alex

Drach, carries a $1,000 roll in his pocket that is "ready to be converted to pounds sterling at the woosh of a jet engine."[37] It is unfortunate that many art security specialists have little but a title by way of expertise. The hope is that this situation will be avoidable in the library and archival world.

Finally, the *Library Security Newsletter* changed its format and title in early 1980, when it began appearing as the journal *Library and Archival Security*.

NOTES

1. "Inventory: Report of the ALA Committee on Library Administration," *ALA Bulletin* 3 (1909), pp. 207-208.
2. "A New Kind of Inventory," *Library Journal* 42 (May 1917), pp. 369-371.
3. American Library Association, "Inventory, Insurance and Accounting." In *A Survey of Libraries in the United States* Vol. 4, pp. 119-131.
4. "Frequency of Inventory," *Library Journal* 52 (September 1, 1927), pp. 827-828.
5. Ralph Munn, "Problems of Theft and Mutilation," *Library Journal* 60 (August 1935), pp. 589-592.
6. Ruth Anne Bean, "Theft and Mutilation of Books, Magazines, and Newspapers," *Library Occurrent* 12 (January-March 1936), pp. 12-15.
7. Randolph G. Adams, "The Character and Extent of Fugitive Archival Materials," *American Archivist* 2 (April 1939), pp. 85-96.
8. Lawrence S. Thompson, "Notes on Bibliokleptomania," *The New York Public Library Bulletin* 48 (September 1944), pp. 723-760.
9. Robert H. Hand, "Defense of Archives Against Human Foes," *American Archivist* 19 (April 1956), pp. 121-138.
10. American Library Association, Library Technology Project, *Protecting the Library and Its Resources: A Guide to Physical Protection and Insurance*, p. 3.
11. John N. Berry, "To Catch a Thief," *Library Journal* 90 (April 1, 1965), pp. 1617-1621.
12. Robert F. Clark and George Haydee, "Your Charging System: Is it Thiefproof?," *Library Journal* 91 (February 1, 1966), pp. 642-643.
13. G. C. Elser, "Exit Controls and the Statewide Card," *College and Research Library* 28 (May 1967), pp. 194-196.
14. Ernest E. Weyhrauch and Mary Thurman, "Turnstiles, Checkers and Library Security," *Southeastern Librarian* 18 (Summer 1968), pp. 111-116.
15. Norman Vinnes, "Search for Meaning in Book Thefts," *School Library* 18 (Spring 1969), pp. 25-27.
16. Maxine H. Reneker, "Study of Book Theft in Academic Libraries," Master's thesis, University of Chicago, 1970.
17. *Survey of Theft Detection Systems*, Library Technology Report, July 1970.
18. Burns Security Institute, *National Survey on Library Security*, p. 27.
19. *Theft Detection Systems for Libraries: A Survey*, Library Technology Reports, May 1974.
20. Lawrence S. Thompson, "New Reflections on Bibliokleptomania,"

Library Security Newsletter 1 (January 1975), pp. 8-9.
21. "Archival Security Surveys," *Archival Security Newsletter* 1 (July 6, 1976).
22. *Security Register*, Vol. 6, Society of American Archivists, November 1976.
23. Donald Bruce Robinson, "A Survey of the Attitudes Toward and Utilization of Security Measures in Selected Academic Libraries," Unpublished Ph.D. dissertation, Florida State University, 1976.
24. Timothy Walch, *Archives & Manuscripts: Security*, p. 30.
25. "Missing Books Section," *AB Bookman's Weekly* 61 (July 11-18, 1977), p. 280.
26. Ibid.
27. Lawrence Thompson, *Robert Frost: The Early Years: 1874-1919*, pp. 372-373.
28. Lawrence Thompson, *Robert Frost: The Years of Triumph: 1915-1938*, p. 37.
29. Alice Harrison Bahr, *Book Theft and Library Security Systems: 1978-1979*, p. 126.
30. Richard Phalon, "The Game Where Nobody Loses but Everybody Loses," *Forbes Magazine*, April 16, 1979, p. 55.
31. David Aikman, "In New York: Reading Between the Lions," *Time*, October 8, 1979, p. 18.
32. "New and Noteworthy," *New York Times Book Review*, October 14, 1979, p. 55
33. Ibid.
34. James R. Mellow, "Monet and Mayhem," *New York Times Book Review*, November 4, 1979, p. 15.
35. Newgate Callendar, "Crime," *New York Times Book Review*, November 4, 1979, p. 24.
36. Robert Schnare, Private interview at West Point, November 2, 1979.
37. Mellow, p. 15.

The thief is sorry he is to be hanged,
but not that he is a thief.

Thomas Fuller, 1732

THIEVES

The art or manuscript thief is not generally poor or uneducated. In fact, such persons are connoisseurs of art or manuscripts. They study assiduously, and many become notable experts in their field. While they are thieves, they are highly educated and elegant thieves. As Edward Moat recalls in his *Memories of an Art Thief,*

> Over the years I had been building up my research library, I had often times wondered if perhaps I was pushing just a little too much money into the shelves. But when this kind of thing comes through, it made the investment, which I think totalled well over twenty thousand pounds, pay off.[1]

Prior to his self-imposed retirement, Edward Moat was one of the most successful art thieves on three continents. In this passage Moat speaks of his own research library. The figures he presents are all the more startling when it is remembered that the time of which he speaks is before the devaluation of the pound. Moat and others like him not only appreciate the finest of art, but are also highly knowledgeable regarding it.

Moat stole both for sale and for his own collection. He was totally absorbed in his work, and that there was a thrill for him in the commission of his crimes in undeniable. Moat does not disguise what he has done. The pride of the craftsman appears when he discusses his work. The reader may wonder if he will ever return to his old trade. Moat is indecisive on this point: "I think now that I shall retire, or shall say I think I'll retire."[2]

Reading Moat's book of his experiences, one is struck by the care and diligence with which he searched for items he considered worth stealing. Particularly interesting to Moat was a painting,

"The Blessed Virgin and Child Enthroned with Saints and Angels," by Gheeraert David (1848). He tells how, after researching the provenance of the work and tracing it from one villa to another, he finally came upon it. Rather than sell it to his patron and some-times fence, he made the man and his bride a wedding gift of it: "I'll tell you why Robert. You and I have been good friends and done good business together. That's a little present from me to you and Teresa."[3]

In such a gesture there is surely more than a touch of the romantic spirit. Yet while Moat prided himself on never using violence, he was not always as fastidious as he thought himself, and there were occasions on which, in order to make good his escape, he came perilously close to losing this boast. It is easy enough to think that here is a kindly old man retelling his life. The fact is that he was a competent art thief, and his crimes were not mere foibles but actual crimes.

Martin R. Strich and Ted Donson were thieves of another sort. They gained access to manuscripts and rare prints by posing as re-searchers. Both relied on the genteel nature of the art and manu-script departments of major research facilities to escape undetec-ted. They were in fact confidence tricksters. Each took great pains to make himself well known in the institutions he victimized and to build up a relationship with the staff in these institutions. Security officers agree that it is the person who is known to the staff and who is respected by them that is many times the greatest security risk. It is by no means unheard of for a university profes-sor to steal books and other materials from libraries.

The case of Martin R. Strich left a legacy of hard feelings. There are many opinions as to what happened. Strich stole a number of Thomas Jefferson letters and other materials from the New York Public Library. Charles Hamilton in his *Scribblers and Scoundrels* relates one of the sadder consequences of the Strich theft, the sui-cide of a manuscripts librarian. He suggests, moreover, that the security officer who caught Strich was dealt with unfairly by the New York Public Library.[4]

Strich was not a particularly clever thief, but he did manage to deceive the manuscript department with his virtuoso performance as a gentleman researcher. Hamilton, to whom he sold the stolen manuscripts, describes him in a somewhat florid way: "Strich was obviously well educated. In the afternoon sun that poured through my window and gilded his features, he seemed almost like some ancient Aztec god."[5]

Posing as an agent for the unidentified owner, Strich offered letters signed by Jefferson and Franklin. Hamilton purchased them, but was suspicious of their origin. He sent his wife to do some checking at the New York Public Library; she reported that the library had no knowledge of the Jefferson letters. Hamilton then called David Means, Manuscript Librarian at the Library of Congress, and was told that the letters were owned by the New York Public Library.[6] Hamilton then contacted the New York Public Library. "It took the library about an hour to find and check the pencilled slips on which was recorded the only evidence of their ownership of these historic documents.[7]

Hamilton, who had paid $1,864 for the documents realized that he had been duped and went to the New York Public Library, where he saw Edward Morrison, of whom Hamilton writes: "His lips quivered, and his voice broke as he described how Strich had fooled him into turning over important files for examination."[8] Then, after it was suggested that Hamilton be more careful in purchasing letters, Hamilton, as he tells it, exploded in righteous indignation at the implication that he was careless while the library was not.

After reporting this incident, Hamilton continued that he was amazed to find that Strich had given his correct name and address on the slip he had signed at the library. Hamilton should not have been amazed, for Strich, like others, knew that if he was caught after having used a fraudulent name or address, he would be charged both with theft and with use of a forged instrument.

According to Hamilton, the detective who had been assigned to apprehend Strich on his return home that evening left duty at 6:00 P.M., at which point the detective's place was taken by a New York Public Library security officer named McKearnin.[9] McKearnin saw Strich returning and called the police and then Hamilton, who went to the police station. Ultimately, Hamilton was permitted to speak to Strich.[10]

Strich later conveyed a remarkable story to Hamilton. He said that in conversation with a man he had never seen before, the other had mentioned how easy it would be to steal something from the library. His first theft was carried out by merely stuffing some letters into a folder. A few days later he returned and took the Jefferson and Franklin letters.[11]

The upshot of the matter was that Strich returned the money to Hamilton, pled guilty, and received a suspended sentence.[12] Although this incident occurred in 1958, the pattern of sentencing for offenses such as Strich's has not radically changed.

It is possible to take exception to some of the details of Hamilton's account of the Strich affair. One is the assertion that ownership of the letters appeared only on one pencilled slip of paper. This is clearly not true. Nevertheless, this account illustrates the ease with which documents can be secreted and removed from many manuscript facilities.

Yet, there is a nagging problem, specifically, the manner in which Charles Hamilton tends to bring his wrath down upon the New York Public Library. Clearly, anyone who understands the nature of a manuscript collection would find many of Mr. Hamilton's statements remarkable. For example, there obviously was more than one place where the nature of the materials was recorded. Further, a letter is identified by its content and nature as well as by its provenance. Anyone can cut off an identity stamp, but nature and content cannot be masked. If someone arrived with an armload of the letters of Philip Schulyer, one would be wary, since the papers of Philip Schulyer reside at the New York Public Library under the care of the keeper of manuscripts.

Other slightly variant accounts of the Strich matter appeared elsewhere in the press. The *Daily News* of May 3, 1958 reported that Strich was charged with grand larceny and that "police said he is the son of a wealthy furniture manufacturer."[13] It continued by saying the Hamilton "exposed the thefts after buying nine of the documents."[14] The *New York Mirror* carried the same article with a change only in the title of the piece, as it was written by the same reporters, Natalie Tiranno and Milton Chernin.[15] The *Mirror* of May 3, 1958 reported that Strich had convinced the Keeper of Manuscripts, Robert W. Hill, that "he was writing a book, one chapter of which would be about the treasures in the library."[16] Laurence Barrett's account for the *Herald Tribune* was as follows: "A furniture salesman who convinced public library officials that he was a scholar filched twenty-one autograph documents of early Federal vintage from the library last Friday and early this week police said yesterday."[17]

Hamilton, and others by implication, advanced the idea that such valuable documents should not have been brought forth. A frequent suggestion was that photocopies be produced in place of the orginals in cases of the sort. Francis Keally, president of the Fine Arts Federation, said in a letter to the *New York Times* of May 10, 1958:

> Would there be any merit in having all the rare letters such as the ones which were purloined photostated in their exact sizes? These reproductions could be used freely for general reference. For the recognized scholar only, the originals would become available.[18]

The response of Keeper of Manuscripts, Robert W. Hill, was published in the May 19, 1958 edition of the paper:

> The vastness of this library is not easy to comprehend. The manuscript division has some 8,000,000 manuscripts. Each of these is, obviously, unique and if lost could not be re-placed. Admittedly some are more valuable than others. To take a purely arbitrary figure, if only one manuscript out of every ten were considered important, photostats of these would approximate nearly half a million dollars in cost.
>
> Even so, we would still be faced with the task of isolating the "recognized scholar" for whom we must keep the originals available. This is precisely the situation we are in now.[19]

Hill was not defending himself, for he had characterized Strich as "well dressed, well spoken, and knowledgeable."[20]

NOTES

1. Edward Moat, *Memories of an Art Thief*, p. 183.
2. Ibid., p. 240.
3. Ibid., p. 195.
4. Charles Hamilton, *Scribblers and Scoundrels*, p. 163.
5. Ibid., p. 147.
6. Ibid., p. 152.
7. Ibid., pp. 152-153.
8. Ibid., p. 154.
9. Ibid., p. 157.

10. Ibid., p. 160.

11. Ibid., p. 161.

12. Ibid., p. 163.

13. Natalie Tiranno and Milton Chernin, "Rare Notes are Stolen," *New York Daily News*, May 3, 1978, p. 3.

14. Tiranno and Chernin, "Rare Notes," p. 3.

15. Tiranno and Chernin, "Rare Letters Stolen," *New York Mirror*, May 3, 1958, p. 3.

16. Tiranno and Chernin, "Rare Notes," p. 3.

17. Laurence Barrett, "Library 'Scholar' Steals 21 'Priceless' U.S. MSS," *New York Herald Tribune*, May 3, 1958, p. 3.

18. Francis Keally, Letter to the Editor, *New York Times*, May 10, 1958, p. 20.

19. Robert W. Hill, Letter to the Editor, *New York Times*, May 19, 1958, p. 22.

20. Barrett, "Library 'Scholar,' " p. 3.

Books are sepulchres of thought.

Henry Wordsworth Longfellow

BOOK THEFT

The scarcity and great effort of time and labor necessary to produce books in past centuries caused the community to look upon book theft as a serious crime. Richard De Bury wrote in *The Philobiblon*: "This sort of sacrilege ought to be prohibited under pain of anathema."[1] And indeed the warnings which sometimes graced bookplates were as stern as De Bury could have wished. This example from 1640 is typical:

> My Master's name above you se,
> Take heede and therefore you steale not mee;
> For if you doe, without delay
> Your necke for me shal pay.
> Looke doune below and you shal see
> The picture of the gallowstree;
> Take heede therefore of thys in time,
> Lest on this tree you highly clime.[2]

The hapless individual who found himself caught in such a situation could obviously expect little mercy. In later years such extreme punishments were softened. But the stigma of the crime remained.

Charles Burney, the great English musical historian of the eighteenth century, had a son also named Charles. This son, the Reverend Charles Burney, D.D., became a noted classical scholar whose rare book collection was such that it was purchased by the British Museum.[3] Yet the younger Burney had been labeled a book thief during his days at Cambridge. The lad had been attending Cambridge when his crime was discovered. There exists a letter

written by one William Cole to his friend John Smaith, Master
of the College, regarding the incident:

> He However ocasinall got back in Mr. Tilliard's Home, &
> sending them back, on some Ocassion, the Man observed that
> several Books were misplaced. & in searching for them that a
> great Number had been taken away, chiefly classical Books of
> Elzevir Editions; wherupon he began to suspect Mr. Berney,
> & complained to Mr. Whisson the under librarian who advised
> him to be quiet and to try and get into his chambers, & see if
> he could discover any of the lost Books: the Bedmaker said it
> would be difficult as her Master was very studious & hardly
> even 20 Minutes out of his Room at a time except at Dinner
> Time: he got in at that Time & found about 35 Classical
> Books in a dark Corner, which he had taken the University
> Arms out of, & put him over in there place and the Tutor
> being spoke to, he went into the Hall, the Day it was first
> discovered to him and then disappeared & this Week a Box of
> Books belong to the Library are sent From London whither
> he had sent them. What further will be done is unknown. I
> pity his Father who must sertainly feel the stroke on the
> young man who can never appear again at the University or
> so his view will be utter overturned.[4]

Despite his father's eminence, the youth was expelled. Cole
expresses sympathy for both the young man and the father. It is
clear, all the same, that the gravity of the offense had appalled
him.

A later instance of book theft involves Whitaker Chambers,
Alger Hiss's nemesis. Keyes Metcalf discharged Chambers from the
New York Public Library when, upon examination of his locker
(staff members understood that lockers could be opened by a
master key for inspection), numerous books taken without authorization from the Columbia University Library were found. Chambers was a Columbia student. In addition, evidence of attempts to
destroy the identification marks was found in his locker.[5]

The notion that book theft is a crime deserving of prosecution
came into existence early. In 1897 a student named Friedman was
caught stealing books at the New York Public Library. The trustees decided to prosecute the youth in the courts. As a result, the

trustees found themselves being pilloried by the press and the public. The student was befriended by the Society for the Aid of Jewish Prisoners, and philanthropist Jacob Schiff personally intervened in his behalf. The result was that Schiff convinced the magistrate that the matter was being handled in too harsh a manner. The young student was fined twenty-five dollars.[6] Later, in writing to Director John Shaw Billings regarding another such situation in 1904, the eminent lawyer and library trustee John L. Cadwalader noted that the same magistrate who had handled the Friedman case might again be involved and again fail to mete out what he felt was adequate punishment. Cadwalader was clearly a man who did not believe in tempering justice with mercy.

Although installation of an attendant to patrol the public reading rooms occurred in 1901,[7] thefts and mutilations continued. Weighing the expense of hiring another attendant against the loss rate, it was decided in 1913 to appoint what was called a "special investigator" to recover stolen materials and apprehend culprits.[8] Today there are a number of people who still occupy this position at the New York Public Library.

The fact that libraries have been made increasingly more accessible to the public is certainly a laudable advance, and one that nobody will gainsay. The fact that library thefts continue to grow is nevertheless disturbing and becomes more so as book prices climb. Technology which deals in at least perfunctory fashion with theft problems has been introduced. Yet the aim is not to catch the thief; it is rather to deter thievery. Commenting upon the use of electronic security devices, Nassau County Library System Technical Services Director Pleasent W. Martin states: "We never accuse anyone of theft. We always say they've most likely forgotten to check out."[9] One quarter of all the public libraries in Nassau and Suffolk Counties have installed electronic theft detectors, currently costing about $15,000 apiece, to stem a 10-percent pilferage rate. The systems are good investments. Robert Sheridan, Suffolk Cooperative Library System Director, states: "If a library is spending $100,000 on new books, it can figure on a good percentage of this amount's walking out the door and never coming back."[10] Thus, the libraries recognize the problem, but they deal with it in a "civilized manner." They never, for instance, will level an accusation of thievery against anybody, for fear of unpleasant repercussions. Such niceties evidently did not hold in the days of Billings and Cadwalader.

Indian library scholar Badri Prasad says that stealers and mutilators of library materials should be punished but feels that it is punishment enough in most cases to deprive the offender of his or her library privileges.[11]

Others opt for sterner measures. The Iowa Legislature, for instance, passed legislation in 1979 which states that anyone caught trying to pass the checkout desk with concealed material from the library will be considered guilty of theft and liable for criminal or civil prosecution.[12] The conspicuous posting of this new law, it is hoped, will stem the rising tide of thefts. One part of this law may well be a problem in that it gives library staff authority to detain "for a reasonable length of time"[13] those suspected of concealing library materials.

NOTES

1. Richard De Bury, *The Philobiblon*, p. 2.

2. Lawrence S. Thompson, "The Biblioklept Curses," *Library Security Newsletter*, November/December 1975, p. 8.

3. "Charles Burney," *Encyclopedia Britannica*, Vol. 4, pp. 853-854.

4. Ralph S. Walker, "Charles Burney's Theft of Books at Cambridge," *Transaction of the Cambridge Bibliographical Society*, Vol. 3, Part 4 (1962), p. 314.

5. Keyes DeWitt Metcalf, *Random Recollections of an Anarchronism*, pp. 158-159.

6. Phyliss Dain, *The New York Public Library: A History of its Founding and Early Years*, pp. 112-113.

7. Ibid., p. 113.

8. Ibid.

9. Ellen Mitchell, "Libraries Tighten Book Security," *New York Times*, July 22, 1979, p. L13.

10. Ibid.

11. Badri Prasad, *Book Thefts*, p. 22.

12. "Iowa Throws the Book at Thieves, Delinquent Patrons," *Library Journal* 104 (August 1979), p. 1510.

13. Ibid.

Our whole dignity consists in thought.
Let us endeavor, then, to think well:
this is the principle of ethics.

Blaise Pascal

THE ETHOS OF ETHICS

The nature of the clandestine or double market of which mention has been made forms the nucleus of the problem with regard to the return to the rightful owner of stolen materials. Naturally, if a person steals items for his or her own collection and does not sell the items, restoration of the materials is seldom accomplished.

The thorny question of the reproduction of specific books, manuscripts, and archival materials, which may be considered a form of theft, is one with which this work shall not deal. Suffice it to say that the following statement of Robert Penn Warren should be given serious consideration: "As for my own letters or manuscripts, if anyone quotes anything whatsoever without my permission, I promise to sue him from hell to breakfast and back by slow freight if I can get a lawyer to take the case."[1]

The fact of the matter is that possession of a physical item does not carry with it the right to publish the contents of this material. The very use of the term *publication* with regard to manuscripts is far-reaching in the legal sense of the term. According to Leslie J. Schreyer:

> When the Copyright Revision Act becomes effective generally on Jan. 1, 1978, statutory copyright protection will apply to letters and manuscripts whether "published" or "unpublished"; and the author (and his estate, heirs, or transferees of the copyright) will have the exclusive right to control reproduction of the work as well as certain types of "public

display" of the work, subject to the doctrine of "fair use" which permits other persons to make "fair use" of the copyrighted work.[2]

The issue of stolen materials may be considered from a variety of points of view. What of the hapless collector who purchases in good faith a piece of material which is stolen? "It is a legal maxim that a thief cannot pass title to a piece of property,"[3] writes Leslie J. Schreyer. In this case, the purchaser, once the theft was uncovered, would have to return the document to the rightful owner. The buyer does have the option of suing the seller to recover damages. The process can, of course, continue from collector to collector, and so on, depending upon the number of parties involved. Despite all the safeguards, the ultimate protection for the buyer stems from the fact that he or she is dealing with a reputable dealer. The dealer's reputation is of importance, and many cases are settled without the need for litigation, since the dealer wishes to protect his or her name and standing in the community in which business is conducted, according to Schreyer.[4]

In the end, what is done with important materials has much to do with the ethical outlook of the person who has possession of them. This is especially true, says John F. Reed, with regard to items of great value:

> Although the owner of manuscripts has the legal right to destroy or alter them at his discretion, if the manuscripts are historically important, he has a moral obligation not to do so. The occasional practice of some dealers and collectors of detaching from a letter a franked address leaf in order to sell it separately is most reprehensible.[5]

The price set for a piece of material can depend upon the dealer's knowledge of the material's value or the seller's ignorance of this value. Dealers who complain about sellers who go shopping for better prices than they themselves offer are advise to examine their own actions:

> Should not a dealer or collector be at least required to tender a reasonably decent price, based on resale value, for any material offered to him? This suggestion has purposely

been presented in the form of a question, since some dealers and collectors may reason that since their knowledge is valuable to them, it is therefore proper, both morally and legally, to take advantage of the lack of knowledge of the novice vendor—a sort of reverse of the "let the buyer beware" theory.[6]

Fraud is of a more insidious nature than the simple, white-collar variety of theft. Such fraud as the forging of merchandise or the selling of stolen merchandise creates an untenable position for the unsuspecting institution that receives the merchandise. As the American Society for Industrial Security's *Guide to Security Investigation* warns, "This form of fraud places a business in the rather untenable position of creating a defense against a problem or condition over which there is no control and that has already occurred."[7]

It should not be assumed that because a person is basically honest he will not steal or endeavor to commit a fraud. If the opportunity presents itself, ". . . there will always be basically honest people who, under certain circumstances, if given the opportunity, will steal."[8]

Steal—the very word has a nasty sound to it. It is hardly to be suggested that the dealer or collector who uses superior knowledge to acquire a bargain is stealing. Expertise in any area commands a price, and this is so certainly in the area of the fine arts. Moreover, as Donson points out, this particular brand of expertise influences art prices in general:

> The art world thrives on appearances; it is the aura of authenticity, which radiates until a piece is unmasked, that attracts the tremendous sums that the art-buying public pays for works of art. The identification of a deception drains the splendored thing of all enchantment; consequently, of all monetary value. Paradoxically, therefore, just as good shines brighter when juxtaposed with evil, the manufacture of fakes, forgeries, and facsimiles in fact *serves* the art world by making a virtue of connoisseurship. The uncovering and denunciation of spurious works of art sustain and reinforce the prodigious spiritual and monetary value which the art world attaches to that intangible—authenticity.[9]

It is invidious to suggest that everybody who buys art works is beset by the "wheeler dealer" mentality—the attitude that he or she must get a bargain at all costs. Nor is it true that dealers automatically attempt to cheat their customers. The usual ground rules, however, fail to hold in the case of stolen art. Here the niceties are thrown to the winds, and "wheelerdealerdom" comes into its own. Greed manifests itself in the behavior of the buyer, as well as in that of the seller. What happens is instructive, as the art in question may be sold at a fraction of its true value, but that value cannot, of course, be realized by the buyer without involving himself or herself in great difficulty.

Art is sometimes smuggled from one country to another. When this happens, there is seldom a legal means by which the art can be brought back to the country of origin. To the charge that Norton Simon had been buying art smuggled from India, for instance, the response was that, as the art work had not been smuggled into the United States, no American laws had been broken.[10]

Bonnie Burnham points out that in New York, plea bargaining can involve the return or recovery of stolen objects. By allowing an accused person to plead guilty to a lesser crime, she says, not only are many cases removed from the jurisdiction of the criminal courts, but also much stolen property is returned to its rightful owner.[11] Clogged court calendars in large cities are, it is clear, a factor that works in favor of recovery.

The law is, of course, a morass, and sometimes its moral effect turns out to have greater importance than any of its actual edicts:

> The law does not, therefore, always act either as a forum for establishing the validity of ownership or as a standard for deterring the loss of important works. An unofficial moral imperative in the art community, however, often functions in the place of effective sanctions to settle questions which might otherwise be caught in a morass of conflicting jurisdictions and interpretations. In the past five years, most of the prominent disputes of ownership centering around bona fide purchase of stolen items have been settled without litigation. This is particularly the case if an object has disappeared from a public institution or monument, or is registered as a national treasure in the country of origin, since such claims are generally recognized throughout the world.[12]

What of objects that are stolen and never reappear? There is always hope that eventually, if only in the far future, these will again surface. Instances in which art objects are recovered after a long delay are fairly common. The Mona Lisa was stolen from the wall in the Louvre in 1919 by a house painter. Two years later the culprit turned himself in, stating that it had been his intention to repatriate the painting to Florence, where it belonged.[13] Such thefts have occurred throughout history. The Greeks are not overjoyed at the fact that thousands of pieces of their best sculpture from the Parthenon are to be seen at the British Museum. Lord Elgin, who removed the sculpture from Athens in the nineteenth century, is seen by many Greeks as a thief who "looted" their national heritage. The revelation about the Canervon-Carter machination with the Metropolitan Museum, thereby allegedly cheating the Egyptian government of its treasures, is only now coming to light.

A disturbing trend is seen in the fact that art thieves are no longer working by stealth and cunning. The armed robbery of museums was highlighted by the December 2, 1973 robbery of the Fogg Museum of Harvard by five men who stole in excess of one million dollars worth of Greek and Roman coins.[14]

It is suspected that some art thefts are being carried out to "fill orders" for culture-prone speculators. Norman Pegden couples the emergence of the cultural speculator with the varying attitudes of governments who have either had their national treasures plundered or who have plundered the national treasures of others:

> Had this property transfer between cultures been a balanced one, then the first argument may well have had some meaning, but as the facts exist the second is nearer the truth since the cultural object has today assumed an often irrationally high material worth due to its beauty, uniqueness or magic association with some past world or human endeavour. Initially, aesthetic values alone were sufficient to encourage the human instinct to possess, and collectors have in consequence multiplied, but add to this high monetary values constantly in the process of inflation owing to increasing demand and limited supply, and one has the ideal situation for the emergence of the cultural speculator. The reality is then the ever-increasing movement of cultural property away from the

materially poor but often culturally rich countries to those who possess the reverse characteristics.[15]

Taking into account good faith on the part of nations, there is a problem in that, many times an object is not reported stolen. Another problem is that there are not clear, cogent descriptions of the article which has been stolen. There have been attempts within various communities of the professional world to combat these problems. The International Foundation for Art Research publishes the *Art Theft Archive Newsletter*. This ten-times-a-year publication gives updates on missing materials and warns dealers of robbers and thieves who have been using a particular modus operandi, as exemplified in the following description from the Summer 1979 *Newsletter*:

> Since our last *Newsletter*, two more New York dealers have alerted the Archive of visits by the man suspected of stealing the Vienna *Stork's Nest* (V. 5, no. 34). The same man, in the company of a woman, is suspected of stealing a cloisonne *Parrot* and a Directoire *Clock* (nos. 59 and 50 this issue). The man identifies himself as an interior decorator and is believed to be interested particularly in French furniture and European decorative arts.[16]

Another service of the IFAR is the *Art Theft Archive*, which lists and catalogs stolen objects. Cooperation is the key to any such program. Despite the appeals to report thefts, according to Bonnie Burnham of IFAR, between 20 and 30 percent of art thefts still remain unreported.[17]

The Society of American Archivists, supported by a grant from the National Endowment for the Humanities, in July 1975 created a *National Register of Lost or Stolen Archival Materials*. The registration form gives the registrant various options as to use of the information:

> Please indicate how you wish us to use the information you are supplying on this form. Should we _____ make it public in the *Archival Security Newsletter* and press releases with the registrant's name; _____ make it public in the *Archival Security Newsletter* and press releases without the

registrant's name; _____ restrict it to phone inquires on a need-to-know basis?[18]

The editor until recently was Timothy Walch.

A perusal of *A List: Material Lost or Stolen After January 1975* indicates that there is much interest in Frost among thieves. It is curious that two of the volumes were annotated by George H. Browne. Similar thefts were mentioned in the first "Books Missing" section of *AB Bookman Weekly*. These are described in the chapter tracing the history of library theft in professional publications. The SAA entries are as follows:

> Frost, Robert
> Bound vol.; *A Boy's Will*; 1913 (2nd ed.?); London; Bronze cloth, inscribed and signed by Robert Frost "RF w/kind regards May 10, 1915", annotated by George H. Browne; public; Univ. of Virginia Library.
>
> Frost, Robert
> Bound vol.; *Mountain Interval*; 11/1916; New York, 1st issue, inscribed and signed by Robert Frost & with autograph corrections by him on pp. 88 & 93 (?), signed "your always friendly Robert Frost"; annotations by Browne on dedication pg., pp. 11, 62, 88, 89, back end paper; public; University of Virginia Library.
>
> Frost, Robert
> Bound vol.; *North of Boston*; 10/1915, reprint; inscribed by Frost, "Your friend RF of Franconia", Ellen Webster bookplate; public; University of Virginia Library.[19]

There are many books, manuscripts, and art objects which are now in the possession of individuals who keep their possession a dark secret. These materials have vanished in "Nacht und Nebel" never to be seen again. The sad fact is that there is little hope that materials lost or stolen years previously will be returned:

> The provenance of an object may be commonly known. Yet the pursuit of claims of title can evoke a tangle of private property laws that vary in principle and in detail. The net outcome is that criminals are rarely punished and rightful owners frequently uncompensated.[20]

If this bleak outlook is to be ameliorated, there must be a network of cooperation and an increasing understanding of the scope and material of the theft problem.

NOTES

1. Robert Penn Warren, quoted in Leslie J. Schreyer, "Legal Ramifications of Manuscript Collecting," In *Autographs and Manuscripts: A Collector's Manual*, p. 177.

2. Leslie J. Schreyer, "Legal Ramifications of Manuscript Collecting." In *Autographs and Manuscripts: A Collector's Manual*, Edmund Berkeley, Jr., ed., p. 176.

3. Ibid., p. 174.

4. Ibid.

5. John F. Reed, "Ethics." In *Autographs and Manuscripts: A Collector's Manual*, Edmund Berkeley, Jr., ed., p. 192.

6. Ibid., p. 195.

7. American Society for Industrial Security, *A Guide to Security Investigations*, p. 49.

8. Ibid., p. 47.

9. Theodore B. Donson, *Prints and the Print Market*, p. 112.

10. Laurie Adams, *Art Cop: Robert Volpe—Art Crime Detective*, p. 7.

11. Bonnie Burnham, *Art Theft: Its Scope, Its Impact, Its Control*, p. 27.

12. Ibid.

13. Adams, *Art Cop*, p. 1.

14. Adams, *Art Cop*, p. 10.

15. Norman Pegden, "A Comparison of National Laws Protecting Cultural Property," In *Protecting Works of Art*, Gerald Shirar, comp., p. 213.

16. "Bulletin," *Art Theft Archive Newsletter*, Summer 1979, p. 16.

17. Bonnie Burnham, Interview, August 28, 1979.

18. Registration Form, *Society of American Archivist Register of Lost or Stolen Archival Materials*, p. 1.

19. *National Register of Lost or Stolen Archival Materials, List A: 1975-Present*, p. 15.

20. Bonnie Burnham, *Art Theft*, p. 8.

Honor and shame from no condition rise:
Act well on your part,—there all the honor lies.

Alexander Pope

THE LIVELY LAWYER

The mention of Ted Donson brings either knowing smiles or cold stares. The man went to the right schools and was, in 1970, a lawyer with the prestigious firm of Cravath, Swaine and Moore. It was during his employment at this firm that an almost unbelievable series of events occurred. A number of letters written by Jacqueline Kennedy Onassis disappeared from the desk of one of the firm's partners, Roswell Gilpatric. Gilpatric was one of the leading members of the firm and a man with an impressive background:

> ...Yale '28, had been with the prestige-encrusted Wall Street law firm of Cravath, Swaine and Moore since 1931. As a former Under Secretary of the Air Force (1951-1953), this stately personage knew his way around among long knives, the standard weapons in the corridors of the Pentagon. Not an easy man to impress or hoodwink.[1]

Donson would attempt to sell the Onassis letters to Charles Hamilton in February, 1970. The resultant furor was great.

Gilpatric let it be known that the letters had disappeared from a locked desk. The claim was made that Donson had received the letters unsolicited in the mail and that he had attempted to dispose of them through autograph dealer Hamilton. Earlier in 1965 Hamilton had offered for sale a letter by Jacqueline Kennedy written to Mrs. Lyndon Johnson. The letter was genuine, and the circumstances involved no theft. Pressure was put upon Hamilton, and the letter was ultimately returned to Mrs. Johnson. The tactics used against Hamilton, a noted dealer, were described by him as "Gestapoish."[2] Thus, the affair of the second batch of letters sold by Donson would have been a way for Hamilton to gain that which presidential power had taken from him, despite the fact that nothing had been amiss. The February 4, 1970 incident made front page headlines, with the *Daily News* proclaiming, "Lawyer: Dear Roz Letters Went to Dear Dupe."[3]

It was reported that when Ted Donson realized that the letters had been stolen, he returned the $500 to Charles Hamilton. However, by then the District Attorney's Office had become involved. Ultimately, Ted Donson would be fined $100. He pled guilty on a minor charge of not having reported his possession of the letters. More precisely, he had violated a law of New York City: "By keeping property worth more than ten dollars which he did not have authority to take, possess or use." This fine and plea occurred in May 1970.[4] The *Daily News* headline was "Jackie's Letters Net $100." The situation was described by Ted Donson's attorney as "a mistake of youth."[5]

The publicity that the story brought to all parties was not something which such an old-line firm would relish. Having the matter splashed over the pages of the dailies was not in keeping with the image of Cravath, Swaine and Moore. Thus, it would come as no surprise that when Ted Donson again made the headlines, he would be associated with another law firm. Even in his younger days, Ted Donson was known as a print collector. In fact, this was advanced as a reason that the letters of Jacqueline Kennedy to Gilpatric were sent to Donson.

Care must be taken not to succumb to the desire for sensationalism in the matter of Ted Donson. In the Gilpatric matter, he pled guilty to a misdemeanor. The case was not of a serious nature, nor was it one that could bring about his disbarment. Ted Donson was, and is, an unusual person. He practiced as a lawyer and was a devoted collector of prints.

In any event, he made the headlines once again on September 7, 1972, when the venerable *New York Times* ran an article by Gene Fowler: "Lawyer Arrested in Theft of $10,000 in Art Prints." In its opening lines this article chronicled the earlier indiscretion of Donson: "A 34-year-old lawyer who two years ago was convicted of trying to sell personal letters of Mrs. Aristotle Onassis was arrested yesterday and charged with grand larceny in the theft of art prints from the Metropolitan Museum of Art."[6] The charge was grand larceny, and the arrest was made on the steps of the Metropolitan Museum:

> Donson was booked on charges of grand larceny in the Central Park Station. At the time of his arrest, he was in possession of two Durer woodcuts representing scenes from the life of Christ and two Canaletto cityscapes. All belonged to the Metropolitan and were valued at $10,000. Donson was released without bail on his own recognizance.[7]

The arrest was not made by the man whose case the operation had truly been. Detective Robert Volpe, who had pursued the case with his partner Marie Cirile, allowed her to make the arrest. What Robert Volpe did was to stay home and paint. It was as if the arrest were an anticlimax to the work which he had put into his first major case.

Something very strange happened two weeks after Donson's arrest. A series of phone calls led police to two lockers in Grand Central Station, where, on September 17, 1972, thirty-eight art works valued at $200,000 were found in two lockers. Among the items were:

> ...four books of rare prints, one woodcut and 33 prints. Among the artists represented were Picasso, Toulouse-Lautrec, Goya, Miro, Degas and Nolde. Representatives of the museums and library identified them as their property, and put a total value of $200,000 on them.[8]

Nothing had been reported stolen, yet once it was published that the police had recovered these works at Grand Central Station, dealers began to call. By September 18, according to a second article by Fowler, the police had received telephone calls from more than fifty art dealers to inquire about missing items.[9] Interestingly, a few days after the find at Grand Central, a Degas was returned to the Brooklyn Museum, which, according to a spokesman, had not known it was missing. The package had been postmarked September 16 and mailed to the museum. The value of the print, an 8 x 7 1/2", black and white rendering entitled "Aux Ambassadeurs," was placed at several thousand dollars.[10]

The prints found in the lockers at Grand Central had interesting ownerships. Twenty-six were claimed by the Museum of Modern Art, the Metropolitan Museum "tentatively claimed" ten, and the New York Public Library claimed two.[11] The remaining prints were to be shown before a group of dealers.

Clearly, no one knew that they had suffered a loss until the works turned up in police hands. Or if a loss were noted, it had not been reported. The lack of checks and inventory control in museums and elsewhere became apparent, and sadly the problem remains to this day.

Despite claims to the contrary, there was no official connection between Ted Donson and the art works found at Grand Central Station. As reported by the *Times*, "police decline to speculate on any connection between recovery of art works and recent arrest of attorney T. F. Donson (*sic*)."[12] No officially promulgated connection was ever made.

The case of Ted Donson was not to be resolved until the following year. In November 1973, Donson pled guilty to possession of stolen property. He was sentenced to five years' probation on December 6, 1973, with the stipulation that he undergo psychiatric treatment.[13] Soon afterwards Donson was disbarred.

The story does not end here. Other men might have been shattered by such a loss. Ted Donson, however, was not like other men. He turned to his first love—prints and printmaking—and devoted his energies to a masterfully comprehensive work, *Prints and the Print Market: A Handbook for Buyers, Collectors, and Connoisseurs*. The work was published to much acclaim in 1977. There are those who consider it inappropriate that Donson wrote the book and is now in the print field. Robert Volpe is not such a detractor:

> VOLPE: It's funny with people. Many people who called were very upset that he's still operating, etc. He's lecturing, he's doing quite well. I don't see anything wrong with it.
> INTERVIEWER: He's an expert in that.
> VOLPE: I mean if the man is good in what he does or if he has something to offer.

INTERVIEWER: He suffered for what he did, too.

VOLPE: I'm a firm believer in that.

INTERVIEWER: He was disbarred.

VOLPE: Everything we've spoken of is rehabilitation. We call it rehabilitation if a man hasn't committed a crime in one year. Here's a man, well—he didn't do any jail time, he's punished, ...Well he was disbarred. I think that altered the man's life. He's embarrassed considerably. He put his act together and is doing well. I think, you know, it's to his credit. I don't personally believe is hounding people. If they commit new crimes...

INTERVIEWER: That's something else again.

VOLPE: Yes, well that's different.[14]

What the Donson episode did was, in the opinion of Detective Robert Volpe, to sound an alarm:

I think Ted Donson did a service rather than a disservice to the art world. He brought to light the fact what one man could do over a period of years. Working alone undetected. If he was greedy he could have devastated them.[15]

Splashed across the headlines of many papers was the fact that someone could just walk out with prints. If Donson could do it, so could ten other people. It has been suggested that were it not for the Gilpatric incident, the fact that items were missing from the Metropolitan Museum might have gone undetected, but this is by no means certain, as the theft could well have been discovered at the time the usage slips were checked during the late-summer closure of the Museum.

The modus operandi of Ted Donson will not be discussed. Mention was made of this in the accounts of the matter. The methods are not what is important. Access must be gained, and the actual method of the spiriting away of an item is of lesser consequence. Donson, because of who he was and what his intentions were, had carte blanche in numerous facilities. He was a regular. It is the regular patrons of whom security professionals are most suspicious and upon whom staffs of facilities tend to look with a benevolent eye.

In February 1977, David Zuckerman, an autograph dealer, was permitted to examine, among other items, the letters of Jefferson contained in the Arents Tobacco Collection. At this time, Zucker-man presented a gift to the collection. The gift consisted of eight tobacco stamps used by state and federal governments in the twentieth century.[16] Who could suspect the motives of a man who contributed to such a collection? Yet David Zuckerman was a thief.

The trail which led to Zuckerman's apprehension was most curious. Known as a dealer, he had been perusing many projects for months at Archives and Manuscripts, New York Public Library. Zuckerman attempted to sell the letters he had stolen to a Long Island autograph dealer, John Fox of Mayflower Auction Sales. The letters he chose to sell Mayflower were signed by, among others, Benjamin Franklin and John Hancock. Fox had given a $500 down payment, pending authentication, for the fourteen letters (Zuckerman was said to have stolen seventy-five letters), for which the total price was $5,000.[17]

What awaited Zuckerman at the Mayflower auction offices on March 14, 1977 was a cadre of police; they arrested him on a charge of grand larceny.[18] Again a trust that had been established was violated. It is to the credit of manuscript keeper Paul Rugen that he pursued the matter, despite the time and effort this required. Rugen told me how helpful the detectives were and that they had shown him every courtesy.[19] A few months later Zuckerman would be wanted on other charges. Eventually he was sentenced, and he is now serving a jail term. His method was to cut the mounting from a bound volume and return the volume seemingly intact.[20] He did not cut the document itself, but rather the binding in which it was held. His depredations con-tinued over a period of months. One thing can be said for Zucker-man—he was very selective in the materials which he took.[21]

The Zuckerman affair only made page 70 of the *Times*. It fared better in the *Daily News*, where a photograph of Zuckerman and the detectives who had arrested him appeared on March 16, 1977.[22]

NOTES

1. Peter Wyden, *Bay of Pigs: The Untold Story*, pp. 314-315.
2. Charles Hamilton, *Scribblers and Scoundrels*, p. 13.
3. Laurie Adams, *Art Cop: Robert Volpe-Art Crime Detective*, p. 43.
4. Ibid.

5. Ibid.
6. Gene Fowler, "Lawyer Arrested in Theft of $10,000 in Art Prints," *New York Times*, Sept. 7, 1972, p. 45.
7. Adams, *Art Cop*, p. 45.
8. Paul L. Montgomery, "$200,000 in Art Works Found in 2 Lockers at Grand Central," *New York Times*, Sept. 18, 1972, p. 30.
9. Gene Fowler, "Stolen Art Owners Sought Here," *New York Times*, Sept. 19, 1972, p. 55.
10. "A Degas, Not Missed, Is Recovered by Museum," *New York Times*, Sept. 20, 1972, p. 93.
11. Ibid.
12. Montgomery, "$200,000 in Art Works," p. 30.
13. Adams, *Art Cop*, p. 48.
14. NYC Detective Robert Volpe, private investigator, Interview, Oct. 12, 1979.
15. Ibid.
16. Bernard McTigue, Librarian-Arents Tobacco Collection, Interview, November 14, 1980.
17. Robert McG. Thomas, Jr., "Theft of Historic Letters from New York Library Laid to Autograph Dealer," *New York Times*, March 15, 1977, p. 72.
18. Thomas, "Theft of Historic Letters," p. 72.
19. Paul Rugen, Private interview, October 5, 1979.
20. Thomas, "Theft of Historic Letters," p. 72.
21. Ibid.
22. "Charged in Library Thefts," *New York Daily News*, March 16, 1977, p. 3.

*I take my seat, with so lofty a spirit and sweet
content that I pity all our great ones and rich
men that know not this happiness.*

Robert Burton

THE NEW YORK PUBLIC LIBRARY

Until late in the nineteenth century, many libraries had little regard for manuscripts. These materials, which became of interest to libraries through the efforts of historians and collectors, were to be found mainly in the files of historical societies and museums further, there were few college-educated library staff members before the turn of the century, and those trained in library schools were a rarity. Only one person of the combined staffs of Astor and Lenox Libraries had attended library school as of January 1896.[1] Manuscripts were the special province of the historian and the collector. Clearly, libraries were little concerned with manuscripts. A decade before, in 1885, Charles A. Cutter has observed: "Hardly anything could show more clearly the distinction between European and American libraries. Instead of being the most valuable part of American libraries, manuscripts hardly exist in them and, moveover, for their chief purposes manuscripts are not wanted there."[2]

The presentation of manuscripts to libraries sometimes caused concern and even consternation. This was especially true if the materials were given by substantial patrons. Nevertheless, those who became involved in manuscript work tended to be persons of some distinction. Though his position was shortlived, A.P.C. Griffin, the first Keeper of Manuscripts at the New York Public Library, possessed credentials. He had been lured from the Boston Public Library for the express purpose of becoming keeper of manuscripts. Hardly a year had gone by, however, before Griffin left, in 1897, to become assistant to the newly appointed Librarian of Congress, John Russell Young.[3]

Griffin's effort had been to begin to create calendars and

to place the manuscripts in some sort of order. Prior to his appointment the manuscripts had been generally regarded as the responsibility of the history and reference departments. It was a gift in 1893 from historian George Bancroft that made possible the purchase of the Lenox Library, which eventually became part of the New York Public Library. Its massive collection was to change the fortunes of a hard-working young assistant librarian, Victor Hugo Paltsits, then assistant head of the Lenox. He was enthralled by the Bancroft collection of typescripts and manuscripts. Paltsits did not have a degree from a renowned institution; rather, he had graduated from an evening school. He would, however, rise to become the State Historian of New York and would ultimately head the new and separate Manuscript Division from its inception in 1914.[4] Through his work the Manuscript Division evolved from a mere curiosity into a major research collection.

Until the great building was completed in 1911, the collections of the Astor and Lenox Libraries remained separate. Paltsits was in the Lenox, where the Bancroft collection had been placed. One can imagine the challenge of the collection. Frankly, many of the staff may well have considered the purchase to be one which would entail endless problems for them.

The attitude of many of the time was that manuscripts were a burden without which a library could easily function. It was an attitude similar to that of the Frenchman who, on being confronted in England, where he had gone to do research, with 1400 folios, spent two hours making notes and then left, indicating to the keeper of manuscripts that he could complete his research without further aid.[5]

Manuscript staffs were generally poorly paid, and their attitude towards patrons would have rivaled that of the sales personnel at a Gucci or Louis Vuitton salon. Shelving was a problem, and there were priorities to be considered. The manuscript was considered by many a piece of ephemera which took time and space that were needed elsewhere.

The interest and dedication which the New York Public Library showed in its work with manuscripts were unique at that time. Having a separate division for manuscripts was the idea of Director John Shaw Billings. He was a great pragmatist, and this was in his view desirable and inevitable:

The development of these special departments was comparatively unknown at the time and represented Billings' characteristically pragmatic approach. Like other librarians of his generation, he had no general fixed theories of library organization and administration, but did what seemed most practical or best suited his inclination.[6]

Unfortunately, he never lived to see the Manuscript Division become a reality. He died on March 11, 1913.

It was on November 16, 1914 that the manuscript Research Room was opened. Victor Hugo Paltsits had been named its director on September 24, 1914. Paltsits had come a long way since his assistantship in the Lenox. He had been State Historian from 1907 until 1911, and he would eventually succeed the great Wilberforce Eames as head of the American History Division.[7]

Keeper of Manuscripts Paltsits would retain his position until 1941. The second Keeper of the Manuscript Division was Robert E. Hill. His tenure was also lengthy. He would serve until 1969. He began his service in the library as assistant to Paltsits from 1932-1936. His next position was that of assistant in the American History Division, which he held from 1936 until he assumed the post of keeper of manuscripts in 1941. His background was in American history, which he had studied at Columbia University.[8]

It was during the tenure of Hill that the publishers' archives, which had been begun by Paltsits, were greatly enlarged. He also garnered many other major items. The extent and significance of these can be gathered by a perusal of the calendars of major collections in the Division.

The third keeper had a brief tenure, in fact, the shortest to date. Gerald D. McDonald replaced Hill in 1969 and remained until 1971. McDonald had begun as chief of the American History Division. His later posts at the New York Public Library were ones of distinction: Acting Editor of Publication, Acting Chief of Map Divisions, Chief of Special Collections.[9] Rather than being trained as an historian, McDonald was a scholar of English literature. His interest in textual criticism and his feeling for the importance of authors' drafts were evidenced in his published works.

Paul Rugen, the present keeper, who succeeded McDonald, is himself an historian. His major at George Washington University was history. He obtained his library science degree from Columbia. Prior to being named keeper of manuscripts, he had worked at the Library of Congress, had been archivist for the Municipal Archives of New York City and an archivist in the Marine Corps, and had assisted in the New York Public Library Manuscript Division.[10]

Each director of keeper of manuscripts has left his mark upon the collection. During the year that Rugen assumed the post, 1971, the papers of H. L. Mencken became available to the public.[11] Rugen realized that the demands of scholarship had to be balanced against the fact that the facility was open to the public, and he has done much to improve security.

As to the security of Archives and Manuscripts of the New York Public Library, it has always been fairly strict. The fact that only the two incidents already mentioned, those involving Strich in 1958 and Zuckerman in 1977, have occurred bears testimony to the sound workings of the facility. Recently, increased care has been taken in the manner in which materials are made available. Now a person is only given one folder at a time, rather than any number of them, as was the case previously. The reason, of course, is that some institutions do not count the items in the folder when it is given out and when it is returned. This is not the case at the New York Public Library; the contents of each folder are counted. Also, a stringent check is made at the signing of the admission card—an arrangement not unlike that used by banks in checking signatures.[12]

The suggestion has been made that society as a whole is becoming larcenous. However this may be, it is true that with determination, a theft can be made from virtually any location, be it bank, library, government office, or whatever. Yet there is a safeguard at the New York Public Library, in that those who use manuscripts are in general known to the staff. The two men who did steal from the collection were accepted as serious researchers; and if the danger of imposters is always present, it is not one likely to present itself often.

Keeper of Manuscripts Paul Rugen firmly believes that thefts, when they occur, should be made known to the world at large and that prosecution should be swift and severe.[13] One kind of person the facility will not admit is the browser, the person who has an active curiosity, but no genuine interest. Rugen recounted a

tale of an individual who rang the bell for the Archives and Manuscripts Room. After the first door had been opened and while the
barred door was still in place, the individual said, "I'd like to see
your most expensive manuscript."[14] Gently, but firmly, Rugen
informed the person that if he had a particular need to use the
facility he would be admitted, but that without such a need, the
facility could not accommodate his request. It might well have
been that the individual was smitten by the idea that in museums
and great libraries priceless treasures exist. The recent King Tut
and Treasures of the Kremlin exhibitions at the Metropolitan may
well have fired his imagination. There are, of course, rare books on
public display in locked cases, and the person may not have
understood the situation.

The locking gates which are at the entrance to Rare Books,
Archives and Manuscripts, and other special collections were
installed in 1930, after three items had been stolen from the
Reserve Book Room, which is known today as the Rare Book
Room. Metcalf discusses these at length in his book *Random
Recollections of an Anachronism*. The thief had been discriminating. He had stolen a first edition of Poe's *Al Aaraaf, Tamberlane,
and Other Poems*, which was then valued at $10,000, a first
edition of Hawthorne's *Scarlet Letter*; and Melville's *Moby Dick*.[15]
Since then no thefts from the Rare Book Room have been uncovered.

A realistic attitude toward security is maintained by Keeper of
Rare Books Lawrence Parke Murphy and his able staff. They do
not allow admittance to people with coats or other such posses-
sions that could be used to conceal books. Time after time, I
have seen the staff direct persons to the checkroom to divest
themselves of such belongings. Items which have been used are
individually checked against the request slips before the gate is
unlocked. Just because there has not been an attempt at theft in
some fifty years does not mean that the staff will become less
vigilant.

The privately endowed Berg Collection of English and American
Literature has, in addition to a locking, buzzer-activated door,
a guard who is stationed between the reading and exhibition
rooms. Dr. Lola L. Szladits, curator of the collection, states that,
to her knowledge, nothing has ever been stolen from the Berg, nor
has an attempt been made to steal anything.[16]

It goes without saying that the security force is of the highest caliber. While surveillance is strict, consideration is given at the same time to the needs and susceptibilities of those who use the materials. If the notion cannot be overlooked that there are those who would loot the treasures of the place, given an opportunity, it is tempered by the knowledge that most users are honest.

The processing and inventorying of every piece of material is an ongoing concern. Despite the fact that there are over eleven million separate items in the collection, a feeling of control and competence is exuded by Rugen and his staff. Remarking on his memories of wading through Melville's *Moby Dick*, Rugen said that little did he realize that one day he would be in charge of the letters and papers of Melville.[17]

An eminent historian, specializing in American history, Rugen mentioned that there is only one period for which the manuscript collection is not as complete as one would like it to be. A gap extends from the Civil War to 1900.[18] It bespeaks the nature of the man that, despite the marvels of the collection, he would indicate an area in which the collection is not all that it could be.

There have been incidents in which persons whom one would never imagine to have an inclination to thievery have purloined and sold documents from the collection. The recent theft and subsequent recovery of $20,000 worth of maps from Yale by a visiting Tulane professor, Andrew Antippas, [19] bear witness to a trend that is unfortunately pervasive. The thieves are scholars who know what they are seeking and how to obtain it. The only hope for the recovery of such items is that dealers will realize they are stolen and inform the involved institutions and the authorities of what is happening. One can hope that a reasonable level of morality holds in this area, as in others.

NOTES

1. Phyllis Dain, *The New York Public Library*, p. 96.
2. Charles A. Cutter, quoted in *The Management of Archives*, by Theodore R. Schellenberg, p. 25.
3. Harry Miller Lydenberg, *History of the New York Public Library*, p. 369.
4. Ibid., p. 428.
5. Kenneth W. Duckett, *Modern Manuscripts*, p. 3.
6. Dain, *The New York Public Library*, p. 122.

7. Ibid., p. 428.

8. Dorothy Ethlyn Cole, ed., *Who's Who in Library Science*, p. 220.

9. Lee Ash, ed., *A Biographical Directory of Librarians in the United States and Canada*, p. 305.

10. Ibid.

11. Sam P. Williams, William Vernon Jackson, et al., *Guide to the Research Collections of the New York Public Library*, p. 46.

12. Paul Rugen, Keeper of Manuscripts, The New York Public Library, Private interview, October 5, 1979.

13. Ibid.

14. Ibid.

15. Keyes DeWitt Metcalf, Telephone Interview, December 16, 1980.

16. Lola L. Szladits, Curator-Berg Collection, Interview, December 15, 1980.

17. Paul Rugen, Interview, October 5, 1979.

18. Ibid.

19. "Yale Security Eyed," *Library Journal* 104 (March 15, 1979), p. 665.

The reason why men enter into society is the preservation of their property.

John Locke

MARKING OF MATERIALS

Manuscripts cannot be readily sensitized as can books and other materials. Their very nature makes such processes unworkable. There are, however, ways in which manuscript materials can be marked. The problem is that many feel that the marking harms the integrity of the document. Another consideration is the cost in time and labor of marking collections. It has been pointed out, further, that markings and stamps can readily be excised by the thief. There are four possibilities regarding marking: perforation, stamping with indelible ink, marking, and embossing.[1]

Each method has its drawbacks, and some of these are more serious than others. There is truly no ink that is totally indelible. It has been suggested that since many libraries discard items without cancelling their stamps, dealers might assume that a work bearing a stamp has in fact been discarded.[2] This is not generally true in the area of manuscripts, but such an assumption can at times be creditable. The use of invisible ink has disadvantages. Invisible ink does work, but a special light source is necessary to view it. Some have suggested that the lack of deterrent value is unlikely to discourage thievery and could even in some circumstances encourage it.[3] Embossing can be partially defeated by means of an iron or pressing. It is of more value when it is used on a particular page of a book. As for perforation, there is concern that this compromises the aesthetics of the piece: "Perforation, however, seems likely to meet with oppostition on aesthetic grounds, particularly as it is necessary to have letters and figures three sixteenths of an inch in height, if a perforating machine is to be used."[4]

Of all the suggestions which have been put forth, the most

interesting comes from two sources in London. Both the Research Laboratory of the British Museum and the Metropolitan Police Forensic Science Laboratory opt for the use in marking of pigments or suitable foils impressed with a countersunk die.[5] There is, however, no commercially available machine or press which will render such a marking.

One reason that the American library community has not accepted this idea may be that perforation and embossing are no longer accepted in the marking of manuscripts. The hand-held perforator, Timothy Walch reports, is no longer manufactured in the United States.[6] Moreover, the custom-made perforator is prohibitively expensive, even if it were decided to use one.

A sorry tale of what can happen to unmarked manuscripts is exemplified in the following scenario. Students at Oxford and Cambridge were found recently to be removing unmarked maps in large numbers from the collections. One such map, a Swiss map of the fifteenth century, was sold in an antiquarian bookstore in the country of its origin. The person in possession of it had died, and his estate was disposed of through the bookshop. There were no markings to give identity, and thus it was sold with the other books and items.[7]

Again, it must not be overlooked that it is generally the contents of a document by which a manuscript keeper can readily identify the document. Yet whether this is always acceptable in a court of law, if there are no markings, is open to debate.

The Library of Congress has an ink which is said to be nonbleeding, nonacid, nonfading, and indelible.[8] This ink is suitable for manuscripts. It is available to recognized institutions in either black or brown from the Library of Congress. The American preference, it seems, is for an indelible ink.

The most perfect marking system is of little use, however, if there are dealers who overlook the ownership, or others who are willing to do the same. There is, however, a deterrent value in the markings, and these do sometimes enable pieces to be recovered more readily without legal complications.

The question of where to place the mark has not yet been resolved. Timothy Walch of the SAA offers the following guidelines:

Above all, the mark should not deface or obliterate any part of the text. If the reverse side of the item is blank, the mark should be placed there. If there is text on both sides, the mark can be placed in any one of a number of locations. Many rare book and manuscript repositories put their marks in the upper right corner of the front of the document. Other repositories, including the National Archives, have placed their marks in the blank space to the right of the salutation in letters or near the heading in other documents, to the left of the complimentary close or signature, in the indentation of the first line of a paragraph, or after a short line at the end of a paragraph.[9]

Assuming that all objects in a collection are marked does not provide as great a deterrent as might be thought. The reason is that the keepers of the collection must know that a manuscript is missing before they can put out an alarm. Nor is there any assurance that the marks will themselves have an effect, as the assumption must then be made that either the thief will not remove them or that the dealer or collector who is offered the material will make inquiries to see if the material has been reported lost or stolen.

It has been argued that many institutions truly do not know precisely what they have in their collections. Merely entering the number of items in a file could lead to the following scenario, as envisioned by Christopher C. Jaeckel of Walter R. Benjamin Autographs:

> Say under the name Ludwig von Beethoven, they simply have the notation on the file card—"3 items." One of these "items" may be a six page ALS describing the composition of his "Moonlight Sonata." But in the records it is simply "1 item." What is to prevent someone from replacing the letter with a steel engraving of the composer? The library still has its "3 items," the thief has a fine new acquisition, and eventually someone, either dealer or private collector, is going to get stung.[10]

Many times I have posited this and other similar scenarios to security people. It was also suggested that forgeries could be put in place of originals. The general answer given was that

replacement would be too much trouble, and certainly unnecessary. There is also the problem that, still today, some collections
will not admit their losses. Recent efforts at replevin have been
fascinating:

> Witness the B.C. West case when the State of North Carolina
> with no record of ownership in over two hundred years
> successfully replevined, with the help of friendly North
> Carolina courts, material last known to be in possession prior
> to the American Revolution. Futhermore there was strong
> evidence that these and/or other similar papers had been
> ordered discarded.[11]

There is a twofold reason that the services of specially trained
people are necessary. A security professional who is grounded in
industrial security, say, may not be aware of the particular problems that confront libraries and archives. Moreover, in industrial
organizations, precautions are taken to guard highly sensitive
materials that would not be acceptable in the other organizations.
For instance, access to certain areas might be restricted and badges
of differing colors required to permit one to move from one area
to another. Such arrangements could not be put into effect unless
the security chief had the utmost confidence of his or her institution. This is generally a rarity. An exception is that of the Brooklyn
Public Library, where Security Chief De Rosa has initiated a series
of area color-coded badges with good results.[12]

It is, of course, possible for specially trained security personnel
to spend part of their time working at tasks not immediately
associated with security. A security official might, for instance,
double as cataloger. The advantages of such an arrangement are
obvious. Joseph R. Volpato, Associate Manager of Security at the
Metropolitan Museum of Art, points to an important one. He
suggests that utilizing security personnel in a dual capacity lessens
budgetary impact and increases productivity.[13]

Again, what we are dealing with is material which can be secreted
upon one's person. Further, the scholars who visit archives are
generally considered above reproach. Yet is it undeniable that
the unique nature of the materials they use can offer unique
temptation. Manuscripts often have great personal appeal, and at
the same time they have an identity that cannot be changed.
Christopher C. Jaeckel writes that every manuscript "can be

described, the description can be circulated, and disposal by a thief can be made very difficult."[14] The assumption is made here that the thief will try to dispose of the material. But this is not always the case. Documents are stolen often enough to enhance private collections rather than for monetary gain. This explains why many stolen items are never recovered. Instead of being sold, they are ensconced in someone's private collection.

One should not assume that only library and manuscript facilities have security problems. It might be assumed that a major exhibition of rare books and manuscripts would be a veritable security fortress. The following, however, is a list of the autograph materials stolen from dealers' booths at the April 1979 Antiquarian Book Fair held in New York City:

> BYRON, George Gordon. Closing three lines of an ALS, 4to, London, Sunday Midnight, Aug. 10, 1806. "I offer 1,000 apologies for the trouble I have given you in this & other instances."
>
> JEFFERSON, Thomas. ALS, smal 4to, In Council, Dec. 8, 1779. He takes "the liberty of laying before the general assembly the inclosed letter and memorial from the Consul of his most Christian Majesty in this State."
>
> ADAMS, John. LS, 1-1/2pp. 4to, Paris, Nov. 1, 1782. To Benjamin Franklin, acknowledging congratulations and discussing peace negotiations.
>
> JEFFERSON, Thomas. ALS, 4to, Monticello, Nov. 7, 1819. To Prof. Constantine Rafinesque, discussing the opening of the University of Virginia and the hiring of Professors.
>
> LAFAYETTE, Marquis de. ALS, in English, 4to, Paris, 1832. To a Dr. Neilson, concerning the cholera plague.
>
> LOUIS XIV. LS, 1/2 p., Versailles, Aug. 9, 1691. To M. de Bisimaux, Governor of the Bastille, granting a pardon to the prisoner Bromfield. Countersigned by Jean Baptiste Colbert.[15]

One dealer, Walter R. Benjamin, has after the above thefts instituted a policy for future shows which may well become de rigueur for the profession:

Despite what we thought were adequate security precautions,

the thief managed to take the letters from our binders during Fair hours, and, quite literally, right from under our eyes. We will, regrettably, have to take further precautions at future Fairs including a ban on the handling of any material without the direct assistance of one of those manning the booth. Needless to say, should any one of the above items be offered for sale we would appreciate being notified so that we may take the proper legal steps.[16]

The admission that the materials were stolen is commendable. Despite whatever security precautions are enacted, there will still be thefts from such shows. This is a sad fact of life. Things are not as they once were, nor, many believe, will they ever be so again. Security will become stricter at such shows, as will the screening of security personnel. And it is likely, too, that security consultants will be hired by the dealers to draw up security methods and procedures for the shows.

The 1980 International Antiquarian Book Fair had stringent security precautions. There was only one entrance utilized, bags and coats had to be checked, receipts were examined as customers left with their purchases, and plainclothes guards circulated. The results were commendable; there were only two reported thefts. As reported in *AB Bookman*:

> . . .two thefts did mar the fair. Leona Rostenberg and Madeleine B. Stern (New York City) reported the loss of Menasseh Ben Israel, *De Creatione Problemata XXX*, bound with Menasseh Ben Israel, *De Resvrrectione Mortuorum Libri III* (Amsterdam: Menasseh Ben Israel, 1635-1636; 2 works in one; thick 12mo.; vellum). The work had been listed in their catalogue at $1,250, and had already been sold.[17]

Libraries and archives are not alone in showing an interest in the marking of their materials. The November 25, 1979 *New York Times Book Review*, an issue devoted to Christmas books, was filled with publishers' advertisements, one of which, on page 90, had the headline "Give the Impression You'd Like Your Books Returned."[18] These words were imposed upon a photograph of a book which bore an impression made by a hand embosser, the same variety used for corporate and notary public stamps. This one was being marketed by an organization named Printemps. The embossment had three initials in its center and around these a legend showing that the book belonged to the library of the owner of the initials.[19] The remainder of the copy read, "Our exclusive hand embosser gives you a library seal with your name and up to three initials. And that makes interesting reading for anyone who borrows your books."[20]

This advertisement occupied one-sixth of a page. Obviously the company selling the embossers believes that there is a market for such a device.

NOTES

1. Roderick Cave, *Rare Book Librarianship*, p. 164.
2. Ibid., pp. 164-165.
3. Ibid., p. 165.
4. Ibid.
5. Ibid., p. 166.
6. Timothy Walch, *Archives and Manuscripts Security*, p. 9.
7. Philip P. Mason, "Archival Security: New Solutions to an Old Problem," *The American Archivist*, October 1975, p. 480.
8. Alice Harrison Bahr, *Book Theft and Library Security Systems: 1978-1979*, p. 106.
9. Walch, p. 9.
10. Christopher C. Jaeckel, "Stolen," *The Collector: A Magazine for Autograph and Historical Collectors* 864 (March 1979), p. 3.
11. Ibid.
12. Frank De Rosa, Private interview, Aug. 27, 1979.
13. Joseph R. Volpato, Private interview, Aug. 16, 1979.
14. Jaeckel, p. 3.
15. Jaeckel, pp. 1-2.
16. Jaeckel, p. 2.
17. Anne McGrath, "I.L.A.B. Fair—The Biggest Ever," *AB Bookman's Weekly* 66:19 (Nov. 10, 1980), p. 3118.
18. "Printemps," *New York Times Book Review*, Advertisement, November 25, 1979, p. 90.
19. Ibid.
20. Ibid.

What is legal and what is ethical are not synonymous.

SEC Chairman Harold M. Williams

THE REPLEVIN CONTROVERSY

Simply stated, replevin is recovery of personal property. The procedure may also be referred to as detinue or claim and delivery. "To recover, the plaintiff must show (1) an interest in the property and a right to both immediate possession and control, (2) wrongful detention by the defendant, and (3) to the extent suffered, any loss resulting in damages."[1]

Replevin is no longer simple. This is especially true regarding ownership of official documents. Henry Bartholomew Cox states that, "There can be no *bona fide* purchaser of a public record. An archive does not need to purchase because it always owned the record in the first place."[2] The case which occasioned this statement was the B. C. West incident. A dealer, B. C. West, offered documents for sale at Parke-Bernet in 1975. Among these were court documents, Hooper indictments, from North Carolina. The State of North Carolina began a replevin proceeding for the documents, an action which was sustained by the Supreme Court of North Carolina. The fact that the Hooper case had been tried in North Carolina caused the North Carolina Court to define the Hooper manuscripts as demonstrably public records not legitimately out of public custody. There were other items of information which North Carolina used in its replevin action. The Hooper indictments had been addressed, for process serving, to one Thomas Frohock. Research showed that Frohock had been given a jail term at the beginning of the American Revolution for failure to surrender his Crown Clerk records to the new state court. The premise of the North Carolina Supreme Court's findings, by which the replevin was successfully completed, was that King George III "would not have knowingly permitted the abandonment of official records."[3]

The indication that Frohock had been a Crown Clerk was intended to establish a history of provenance and ownership. The argument that King George III would never have knowingly abandoned the records carried this point further. Generally, replevin is used when property has been stolen and a person has been wronged. There was no indication that the Hooper materials had been stolen or that any wrong had been committed. Later it was stated that it was believed that the documents might have been stolen. What was happening was that the simple fact was being advanced that no individual could have a right to possession of official records or documents. No longer did there have to be a theft involved—mere possession was grounds for replevin proceedings to be instituted. In this instance, it was sufficient merely to show the chain of ownership from King George III to the courts of the State of North Carolina.

The spectre of the challenging of ownership or replevining of documents may well have a chilling effect on collectors of research materials. Mr. Cox feels that many facilities "will either forbid research to be done from the manuscripts or will simply lock them up permanently."[4] Collectors and others argue over what they may feel is unethical. Replevin actions may well cause some records to be destroyed, as the cost of litigation is large.

The problem is one which is not resolved; its implications on ownership of archival records are far-reaching. Can a state attempt replevin of "official documents" from a major research facility? Captured German, Italian, and Japanese war records which are in the U.S. National Archives could well be considered to be the legal property of their governments. This suggestion is not without precedent. The Bavarian State Government has sought to enjoin the sale of the Herman Goering diaries by Parke-Bernet on similar grounds.[5]

The great interest in historical documents, spurred on by the movement for conservation of archives and manuscripts, may well cause some overzealous facilities to begin questionable replevin proceeding. There is also a feeling among dealers and collectors that rather than reporting the loss or theft of materials from their institutions, archive and manuscript curators will wait until these materials have come on the market or there is a report that they have been sold before bringing about an action for replevin. Dealers and collectors who have bought official documents in

good faith do so at their own risk. So, too, do archive and manuscript curators.

The controversy unleashed by *North Carolina* v. *B.C. West*
could result in a terrible legacy. There has been a suggestion that
federal laws are needed to counteract the present state of confusion. If, on the other hand, each state were to pursue its own
course in the matter, a crazy quilt of lawsuits could result. The
stringent policy of the UNESCO statute on archives may offer
some guidance:

> Any person or private body, not being a dealer, who has in
> his possession documents more than 40 years old must
> notify the director of the national or local archives. Within
> 60 days these must be examined by an archivist and may
> be declared to be of major historical interest. Once so
> declared, the state has the power of surveillance and the
> records automatically become open for research purposes.
> The owner must preserve the records in a suitable manner,
> catalogue and repair them, notify the national archives
> before transferring ownership or custody, and apply for
> permission to export. Deposit is to be encouraged by the
> award of a diploma of merit to the owner, the award of
> scholarships bearing his name, and the promotion of research
> on his documents.
>
> Dealers must notify the national archives of all documents
> in their possession, give 30 days' notice of intention to sell,
> and register the results of all sales, the register to be inspected
> by the archives service. The final provision of the draft allows
> for the expropriation of any documents in the hands of
> anyone who breaks the requirements of the articles relating
> to private archives.[6]

The possibility of abuse in replevin cases is always present. It is
not to be supposed that a thief who sells a stolen document to an
unknowing buyer would be above offering to sell the victimized
institution information as to where and how the piece might be
recovered. The result would be a replevin action in which the thief
himself or herself motivates the action. It might also come to a
point where facilities were offering rewards to persons who

assisted them in successful replevin actions. In this case, dealers and galleries might, of course, cease publicizing what had been sold, and canny buyers might insist upon a written agreement whereby the sale of a piece or the buyer's name could not be divulged. This is a quite common practice in the art world. Often when a work of art is reported missing, the owner's name is not mentioned. The reason for such secrecy is obvious—for security reasons and perhaps others, collectors do not want to let the public at large know either who they are or what they collect. Increasingly, manuscript and autograph collectors who fear for the safety of their collections are following suit.

NOTES

1. Institute for Business Planning, *Lawyer's Desk Book*, p. 341.
2. Henry Bartholomew Cox, "Caveat Emptor: The Ownership of Public Documents," *AB Bookman's Weekly* 62 (Sept. 4, 1978), p. 1244.
3. Ibid., p. 1246.
4. Ibid., p. 1259.
5. Ibid., p. 1256.
6. Kenneth W. Duckett, *Modern Manuscripts*, p. 82.

*In a society where certain kinds of theft are
the common rule, the utility of abstinence from
such on the part of a single individual becomes
exceedingly doubtful, even though the common
rule is a bad one.*

G. E. Moore: Principia Ethica, v, 1903

THE GOOD DOKTOR

There have been instances in which library administrators have seen fit to abscond with part of their library's collections, and there have always been persons who pose as scholars and steal for profit. An amalgam of these two types of criminal behavior, along with a taste for cold-war politics, espionage, and impersonation, infected the character of Dr. Joachim Kruger-Riebow, Director of the Music Section of the German State Library of East Berlin.

The matter began simply with three inches of print in the September 15, 1951 entertainment section of the *Times*: "The priceless conversation books recording Beethoven's talks with his friends during his final years of deafness have disappeared from the former Prussian State Library."[1] Mention was made that Dr. Kruger-Riebow, "who had the reputation of being a local Socialist Unity (Communist) party member until he absconded, is presumed to be working his passage home with these treasures of Germany's musical heritage."[2]

The truth is that Kruger-Riebow had not merely absconded, he had backed a truck up to the library on May 1, 1951 and using the two keys—the only ones of their sort in existence—took four crates of material from the vault. The truck made its way into West Berlin. Ultimately, the doctor arrived with the crates at Beethoven House in Bonn, where its director, Dr. Joseph Schmidt-Gorg, was waiting. The tale that Kruger-Riebow told is that he had managed, at great risk, to spirit these materials from East

Germany since they were destined for Moscow. The overjoyed Dr. Schmidt-Gorg gave Kruger-Riebow an itemized receipt. Among the items listed were the following:

...dozens of letters written by Buxtehude, Czerny, Mahler, Mendelsohn, Meyerbeer, Richard Strauss and Cosima Wagner; two musical manuscripts each of Glinka and Debussy; Handel's *Slave Regina*; twenty-seven Beethoven manuscripts, including sketches for the *Pastoral* sonata, Op. 28, *Missa Solemnis*, String Quartets Nos. 12 and 16, Opp. 127 and 135, respectively; and the Eight and Ninth Symphonies; and, most staggering of all, 137 of the extant 139 "conversation notebooks" to which the deaf Beethoven, during the last decade of his life—a decade that saw the creation of his supreme masterpieces—had to resort in order to communicate.[3]

Kruger-Reibow was hailed as something of a hero, as he had after all given up a fine position to bring these great musical treasures to the West.

He did not return to work as a librarian, but instead opened an antiquarian book business called the Bayreuther Musik-Antiquariat. This business was operated from a post office box, and impressive catalogs began to appear. Items in them went up to as high as $5,000 in price.[4]

For some time all went well with Kruger-Riebow, whose face was familiar in many libraries. What was to befall him eventually was ludicrous. He was detained by a policeman at the Goettingen University Library in Lower Saxony after the policeman had been alerted by a patron to suspicious behavior on the doctor's part.[5] He was searched, and two volumes were found on his person. An estimate of their value was seventeen dollars each. The books he had stolen were *American Book Prices Current, 1956-1957* and *1957-1958*. It was routine that the hotel room of this visiting scholar be searched. Among the contents of his room were "a portable chemical workshop for the eradication of library stamps and other identifying markings"; also there were "literally thousands of slips of paper, each one bearing the title of a rare book and the name of a library where one might consult it."[6]

As if that were not enough, there were two rare books for which the doctor had received money from a Japanese client. These books had been stolen from the Duke August Library in

Wolfenbuttel. One of them was the *Deutscher Liederhort*, by Ludwig Erk.[7] The doctor was arrested in September 1959, but the *New York Times* did not learn of the event until January 28, 1960. The written account in the *Times* by Arthur J. Olsen is perhaps as close as the *Times* has ever come to being sensational:

> The police in Lower Saxony are holding a fifty year old bookseller Joachim Kruger for a fantastic series of crimes. The police tentatively place the value of $5,000,000 on the material stolen partly by single item and partly by the case.[8]

It might be noticed that the name of the doctor has been shortened; no longer is he spoken of as Dr. Joachim Kruger-Riebow, but rather as Joachim Kruger. This is because he was not in fact a doctor. He did, however, have a perfect explanation ready for a cold-war audience. He was given the title doctor, he claimed, by American military intelligence, as he had been a member of a sabotage battalion of the Waffen SS and later joined the Gehlen organization, an espionage network used against the Russians. The Gehlen system was retained and operated after the War by the Americans. The explanation did not make much sense. And there were other difficulties: "His record in Magdeburg shows he had been sentenced on April 23, 1936 to two and half years' imprisonment...[His] crimes involved such human failings as forgery, fraud, embezzlement and theft."[9]

So much for the security checking that the East Germans had done when this man who had not completed his course at the Stendal Gymnasium became their senior curator. Kruger stole books to order for his clients. European justice can be swift and harsh. Kruger was sentenced to eighteen months in jail for the theft of the two rare books and the two books valued at thirty-four dollars.

The manuscript community could hardly wait for him to be charged with the crime of having stolen the Beethoven conversation books, among other important items. The former bookseller again prepared to give his anti-Communist explanation of what had happened. In July 1961, the prosecution began gearing up to charge him with the massive theft from the German State Library. There was a problem. The punishment for theft in West Germany was five years' imprisonment, but as the Statute of Limitations required prosecution within five years of the crime, Kruger would go scot-free.[10] Kruger was charged with shoplifting in 1962. This charge, however, was dropped. Then, in 1963, while similar charges were pending, he disappeared.[11]

What happened to the material that went to Beethoven House? Dr. Karl Heinz Kohler, Kruger's replacement at the German State Library, wrote several letters to Dr. Schmidt-Gorg at Beethoven House. The response of Beethoven House gave reasons why the treasures were never really the property of East Germany. The logic involved in the refusal does not bear close scrutiny. The refusal was "...based on the fact that the Prussian State Library, the original owner of the treasures...ceased to exist in 1945 along with the German state of Prussia; the library changed its name first to the Public Scientific Library, then to the German State Library. . ."[12]

The Director of Music at the German State Library took great exception to the refusal. West Germans of note speak of the differences between anti-Communism and the recognition of common thievery. Ultimately, the treasures were returned to the German State Library.

The stolen manuscripts were valued at $5,000,000. The *Times* correspondent Arthur J. Olsen quoted John J. Fleming, rare manuscript expert, as having said, "That's more than all the known sales of books and manuscripts in the past ten years."[13]

Among the items which never surfaced at this time was a three-part Mozart piano sonata. This never found its way back to East Germany, and there was speculation that Kruger had sold it. Cautiously, the *Times* stated; "Rudolf F. Kallir, who bought the Mozart piano sonata in three movements, said yesterday that he had acquired it from a well-known dealer here in 1955. He said he had received a purported authorization of sale."[14] It was never confirmed that Kruger had sold the sonata to Kallir.

If ever there was cause for a replevin action, it could have been found in a statement by Paul Moor in the March 1977 issue of *High Fidelity*. Here Paul Moor identified the whereabouts of the sonata. According to Moor, it was "in the Morgan Library in New York. The Morgan has it on indefinite loan from the opulent collection of Robert O. Lehman."[15]

A more spectacular story of malfeasance by a library or manuscript administrator has not surfaced. Kruger was a man whose time had not come. He was a superb confidence man, in an age when such activities were not fully given their due. The audacious nature of the matter is mind-boggling. The fact that Kruger was apprehended because he stole two books valued at thirty-four dollars is almost unbelievable. Kruger was sentenced to eighteen months in jail. It is idle to speculate on what would have happened, had Kruger not fled, in the matter of the massive theft from the German State Library, but the supposition is that prosecution would have been precluded by the new German statute of limitations.

The Kruger affair was reported in 1960 in the American press. Little appears to have been done at the time, however, to tighten security in American institutions. Seventeen years later, it was as if manuscript theft had just been discovered. "Now It's a Wave of Theft in Historical Documents," proclaimed a headline in the September 5, 1977 *U.S. News and World Report.*

The article itself contained quotes from Charles Hamilton, Philip Mason, and others. The tenor of these quotes was disquieting. Charles Hamilton was reported as saying: "Librarians put inept people in charge of valuable collections and then scream at dealers."[16] Philip Mason cited the phenomenal interest in genealogy as one factor contributing to library thefts. He suggested also that some unemployed scholars might be turning their talents to theft and that the impact of the new copyright law could cause people to steal materials rather than copy them by hand.[17]

To those who had a knowledge of the field and an understanding of the problem, the article contained no startling news. Although librarians were portrayed in the article as neglectful and thieves as persons of education and standing, it was pointed out with some playfulness that there was no possibility of the Constitution's disappearing from Washington.

Nineteen years after the Kruger thefts and numerous others, the Antiquarian Booksellers Association put together theft guidelines. These were promulgated in the summer of 1979. *AB Bookman's Weekly* listed them in its issue of October 8 of that year under the headline: "Theft Guidelines Now A.B.A.A. Policy." The guidelines are as follows:

1. Members will make all reasonable efforts to ascertain that

materials offered to them are the bona fide property of the offeror.

2. In those cases where the stamp, perforation, or other identifying mark of a currently existing library or other repository is visible, on offered materials, or no deaccession mark or notation is visible, members will make appropriate inquiries to determine the current ownership status of the materials.

3. Members will not knowingly purchase, hold, or attempt to re-sell stolen materials, or items which they suspect have been illegally or improperly removed from the possession and control of any rightful owner.

4. Members will cooperate fully with law enforcement authorities in their efforts to recover and return to rightful ownership any materials that may have been illegally or improperly removed from public or private collections, and will cooperate in efforts to apprehend persons responsible for any thefts of antiquarian books and related materials.[18]

One does not wish to appear cynical. It is useful to point out, however, that honest dealers have always acted decently and can be expected to go on in this way, while the other sort of dealer will just as surely continue in the old way.

Some of the guidelines lack definition. The wording of Guideline 4, for instance, is nebulous. Who is to decide what is "cooperating fully?" Dealers and law enforcement authorities can have differing opinions on what is and is not full cooperation.

Guidelines 5 and 6 are as follows:

5. To assist the public and its members in identifying and recovering stolen materials, the Association has instituted these measures: (a) the Association will distribute immediately to its membership any list of missing or stolen rare books and related materials that is provided to it by the owner or police authorities, providing that the monetary value of each item shall exceed $100 and that the aggregate of each loss shall not be less than $1,000; (b) in cooperation with *AB Bookman's Weekly*, space has been made available in *AB* at modest rates to any individual or library for rapid circulation of descriptions of missing items to the approximately 8,000 *AB* readers.

In addition, any member who is offered materials he recognizes as having appeared in lists of stolen or missing properties, or who suspects that materials offered to him may have been illegally or improperly removed from a public or private collection or another dealer's premises, will immediately notify law enforcement agencies and rightful owners, if known; will attempt to gain possession of and hold such materials pending determination of ownership; and will appear as a witness in actions against suspected thieves.

6. The Association will offer its expert services in the effort to resolve disputes in the determination of ownership of materials alleged to have been stolen.

The Association voices its concern that libraries and others have not consistently been forthcoming in promptly identifying to A.B.A.A. and booksellers in general materials missing from collections.[19]

The final statement in Guideline 6 is important. The problem here, of course, is that often enough no one knows the material is missing until it is in the hands of a dealer or the police. A theft case mentioned in the *AB Bookman's Weekly* on October 1, 1979 provides a good case in point. The article mentions that nine folio art volumes stolen from the State University of New York were uncovered in a Buffalo federal drug raid. "Library officials apparently had not been aware of the theft until local newspapers published an account of the recovery of the items."[20] Once the library knew about the theft, were they willing to give any information to A.B.A.A.? One can surmise the answer from the following report: "While the library declined to furnish information about the theft, a university spokesman informed *AB* that the books were stolen from the special collection in Copen Hall but not the Rare Book Collection, which he said is kept under stricter security."[21]

It would seem that the university spokesman felt that *AB* would only be interested in "rare books" and not in books kept in "special collections." Almost as a throwaway, the *AB* article continued: "Authorities are currently investigating a suspected connection between the stolen books and a former Copen Hall maintenance employee, now under arrest."[22] There is a normal reluctance on the part of institutions to discuss such losses, but it is to be hoped that this reluctance will give way eventually to the need for proper publicizing of losses.

NOTES

1. "'Beethoven Books' Are Lost in Berlin," *New York Times*, Sept. 15, 1951, p. L7.

2. Ibid.

3. Paul Moor, "The Great Mozart-Beethoven Caper," *High Fidelity* 27:3, p. 73.

4. Ibid., p. 74.

5. Arthur J. Olsen, "Bookseller is Accused of Looting Musical Treasures in Germany," *New York Times*, Jan. 28, 1960, p. 11.

6. Moor, p. 74.

7. Ibid.

8. Olsen, p. 11.

9. Moor, p. 75.

10. Ibid., p. 77.

11. Ibid.

12. Ibid., p. 75.

13. John J. Fleming, quoted in Olsen's "Bookseller," p. 11.

14. Olsen, p. 11.

15. Moor, p. 77.

16. Charles Hamilton, quoted in "Now It's a Wave of Thefts in Historic Documents," U.S. *News and World Report* LXXXIII:10 (Sept. 5, 1977), p. 51.

17. Philip Mason, quoted in "Now It's a Wave, " p. 52.

18. Ibid.

19. Ibid.

20. "Drug Raid Nets Cache of Stolen Books," *AB Bookman's Weekly*, Oct. 1, 1979, p. 2054.

21. Ibid.

22. Ibid.

Nothing hurts worse than the loss of money.

Livy

LOST OR STOLEN?

The fact that security considerations have not been given their due in the past makes the task of doing it now all the more difficult. The Doe Library at the University of California at Berkeley had a full inventory in the 1940s. These records were no longer available in 1976 when Neal Kaske researched book thefts at that institution. Before Neal Kaske's work, figures on book losses in the main stacks were determined from an examination of three sources: the ongoing replacement of lost books by acquisitions, a trial stack inventory in 1972, and a service survey conducted in 1969 by the loan department.[1]

The sources which were available at the Doe were more complete than is generally the case elsewhere. The very idea of a stack inventory is anathema in a large library. Even the 1972 trial survey at the Doe was never fully completed.[2] Undoubtedly, such inventories are needed at major facilities, but carrying them out is a practical impossibility.

Many times in speaking to persons about thefts and losses, I would be given an estimate qualified by the phrase "that we know of." The library thief knows that the odds of a book's being discovered as lost or stolen are not great. And, in fact, unless another patron requests the book, the theft may never come to light. This is especially true when the thief also removes the cards from the catalog file. The shelf list is one of the few remaining places where the book would be listed, and the odds against the shelf list's being checked are great.

It is, of course, easier and less embarrassing to report a book as missing rather than as stolen. Also, it is not possible to say that a book has been stolen merely because it is not in its correct place on the shelf. There are always irresponsible patrons who purposely misplace books they are using to ensure that the books will be available to them on a later visit to the library.

Library policies change, and the manner in which materials are handled varies from place to place and from one time to another. The story is told of how at West Point during World War II, a boxcar load of rare books was shipped to the Library of Congress for safekeeping. There were no librarians at West Point at that time, and unfortunately those in charge of the operation neglected to list the books. Whether or not any of them were lost then or later is not known. What is known is that numerous items of which West Point has no knowledge appear in the National Union Catalog. That wartime arrangement no doubt had to take place as it did. It is certain, however, that no such casualness as was demonstrated then would be possible now.[3]

The marking of rare books in the old days at West Point also left something to be desired. Someone there decided that rare books should be identified by placing a large "X" with a yellow crayon on the back of each of them. Special Collections Librarian Robert Schnare mentions that there is a Copernicus incanabula in the collection which bears an ink stamp on its title page reading: "U.S. Military Library."[4]

Librarians often find that the collections they inherit have been mishandled and abused by their predecessors. The level of professionalism in earlier times was often low. And a factor that added to the overall problem is that, until comparatively recently, little was known about conservation.

Materials added in the last five years to a collection are, many believe, among the most susceptible to general theft and pilferage. Neal Kaske believes that the value of these materials may "represent a dollar value equal to or greater than the cost of additional security for the collection."[5] Such materials do not usually attract the attention of the more highly organized thief. Such thefts as do occur tend to be of the "impulse" sort.

Losses that go unnoticed are bound to be sizeable. The estimated dollar value per item, without processing, was placed at twenty dollars at Berkeley's Doe Library. This average figure could, of course, be multiplied many times over in the case of losses from a special collections department. Yet the idea of an inventory is bothersome. Spending money to prove that a library is not as secure as was believed does not seem at first glance a particularly appealing endeavor.

The very fact that no thefts have been discovered can lead to a false sense of security. The downtown Free Public Library in New Bedford, Massachusetts had an alarm system installed to protect its general collection. The new interest in library security had prompted the library to fear for the safety of this collection. Herman Melville memorabilia were displayed in glass cases in the library. These materials were not insured, and there were plans to put in an additional alarm system to protect them. Unfortunately, before this was done, materials whose estimated value was $50,000 were stolen.[7] Not having the materials insured was a mistake, as was certainly the lack of an adequate alarm system. It is felt that a sudden great increase in the use of the library's genealogy collection, which was protected, might have signaled the need for immediate protection of the Melville collection, as the Melville treasures would be seen by crowds of people who had not been in the library previously, and the very presence of large numbers of people would allow the staff little opportunity to observe patrons who were acting suspiciously.

The idea that people do not know the value of what is in a collection is certainly no longer true, if it ever was. Even many without academic training are highly knowledgeable about library materials and their values. People do know about prices. The idea that they do not have such knowledge is certainly erroneous; and even it it were not, this is no reason to ignore security matters. The people who stole 153 volumes from the Carleton College Library in Northfield, Minnesota knew what they wanted and had a knowledge of the value of what they stole:

> 123 titles dealing with the exploration of the New World. Imprints include eight volumes from the Sixteenth Century, one volume from the Seventeenth Century, 61 volumes from the Eighteenth Century, 80 volumes from the Nineteenth Century, and 4 volumes from the Twentieth Century.[8]

An incident which is illustrative of a concern for security concerns the Rockford, Illinois Public Library. In order to gain an electronic security system, this library let is be known that the book thefts from its main building were costing the community $108,000 a year. *The Library Journal* reported the ensuing uproar as follows:

> The announcement drew sharp criticism from the *Rockford Register Star* which in its editorial pages asked why the board took so long to address the problem and hadn't done anything more than to post CETA people at exits as checkers. Another question it raised was why theft is so rampant at the main, while branches don't seem to have the same problem.[9]

It becomes evident that institutions can no longer trot out scare figures with impunity, even when the motive, as here, is a good one. It is equally evident that concealing bad news can have disastrous consequences. If one is inclined to feel that trouble is avoided in this way, the response of the *Rockford Register Star* should be enough to destroy the notion.

Certain collections lend themselves to very strong usage. Topics which are novel, burgeoning, or the province of certain political or socioeconomic groups are generally in demand. A study of the Moffitt Undergraduate Library at the University of California at Berkeley by Neal K. Kaske indicated that the percentage of volumes which had circulated at least once in eighteen months was as follows:

Moffitt Women's Studies — 94.92%
Moffitt Chicano Studies — 94.24%
Moffitt 1976-1977 acquisitions — 72.66%[10]

Problem areas of collections can be identified without much trouble. But one problem that defies easy solution is that of rare books which are kept on the shelves of general collections. It is common enough to find books in a general collection that deserve to be in either rare or special collections. Small New England libraries, until a few years ago, had Frost first editions on their shelves. After a series of thefts, the remaining libraries moved these volumes to safer quarters. If it took a theft to indicate what was valuable and susceptible to theft, at least the problem has now been more or less contained.

The undervaluing of particular titles and types of collections nevertheless remains a problem. Larger libraries tend to have the resources to give their holdings proper attention. It is in smaller libraries, which are old enough to have valuable books but which are not adequately funded to identify these and remove them to a special collection for safekeeping, that the problem continues. And it is compounded in cases where collections are combined, whether as an economy measure or not, making the identification of valued items even more difficult.

Rowland G. Freeman, head of the U.S. General Services Administration, has suggested that a presidential library be established to hold the records of the next six presidents. The plan would save money for the taxpayer and would centralize the holding of presidential papers. The problem would be that with six such collections in one facility, unless each collection were considered a separate entity, there would be even greater problems of security, access, and records management. Freeman felt that the government role should be limited to "archival storage of presidential papers with only a very limited capacity for exhibition."[11] The phrase "archival storage" brings to mind a massive warehouse rather than a series of functioning collections manned by professionals. Such a concept can only give reason for conern.

NOTES

1. Neal K. Kaske, *A Report on the Level and Rate of Book Theft from the Main Stacks of the Doe Library at the University of California, Berkeley*, p. 1.

2. Ibid.

3. Robert Schnare, interview, Nov. 2, 1979.

4. Ibid.

5. Kaske, p. 50.

6. Ibid., p. 54.

7. "The Melville Heist," *Library Journal* 104:994 (May 1, 1979), p. 994.

8. "Minnesota's Carleton College Reports Rare Book Theft," *Library Journal* 104:1097 (May 15, 1979), p. 1097.

9. "Security Shortcomings Assailed," *Library Journal* 104:878 (April 15, 1979), p. 878.

10. Neal K. Kaske, *A Study of Book Detection Systems Effectiveness and the Levels of Missing Materials at the University of California, Berkeley*, p. 7.

11. Rowland Freeman, quoted in "Central Library for Presidential Records Suggested," *New York Times*, Nov. 11, 1979, p. 50.

If we don't solve our own problems,
other people will—and the world of
tomorrow belongs to the people who
will solve them.

Pierre Elliott Trudeau

WEST POINT

Indicating a series of oil portraits, Egon A. Weiss, Director of Libraries of the United States Military Academy at West Point, mentioned why he had had them hung higher on the library walls: "I read that a thief, using a razor-blade, can remove a painting from its frame without damaging the painting in thirty-five seconds."[1]

Many times security becomes a matter of concern only after a theft has taken place. It is then that directors wish the hands of the clock could be moved backward so that security precautions could have been observed earlier. Vigilance may well be the keynote of security considerations at West Point.

Weiss views security as part of his overall responsibility, and he has imbued his staff with the necessary attitude toward security. It is not unusual for him to check doors which should be locked as he goes about the building. He insists that certain doors be locked after a certain hour, and further that the name of the person who locks that door be posted on a chart beside the door.

"Security is everybody's job," Weiss says.[2] A policy exists whereby the janitorial staff will call Weiss at his home if a problem arises. "They know I want them to call me anytime—even in the middle of the night—if something is wrong," he observes. Weiss considers security a prime responsibility of his job, even though security is maintained at West Point, which is a Federal facility, by the Provost Marshall's office. If there were a theft at the Point, this would be investigated by the CID and the FBI, since it would be considered that a federal offense had been committed.

71

The head of Special Collections at West Point, Robert E. Schnare, voices other concerns:

> As far as archives and manuscripts go, we don't have any security problem. What we've lost has been through staff incompetence or misshelving. Or it's been ripped off years ago. Because there has never been an inventory and because access and control could be better, things do go missing.[3]

At West Point, there is no urgency regarding security. Each member has an awareness that security should be an ongoing consideration. Thus, if anything were to threaten security, measures would be taken automatically to deal with the situation. The hallmark of the security program is that schedules are changed, as are methods of operation. There is nothing, especially in routines, upon which a potential thief can seize.

Although it would be easy for the staff to be put off its guard since there are few problems, this would be disastrous from a security standpoint. There is no feeling of complacency. The degree to which the staff involves itself in maintaining security is truly remarkable.

Weiss believes that all thefts should be reported widely. It is his feeling that such reports alert other institutions to the dangers that they face. He has little patience or sympathy with institutions which try to conceal the fact that they have been the victims of a theft.

Donald Koslow, the Assistant Director, feels that the unscrupulous private collector poses a threat, since materials stolen by such persons do not come upon the market.[4] Weiss and Koslow both agree that in the past, little danger existed of thefts by scholars and researchers but that this danger is present today. According to Schnare; "Society is not doing too well either. Times are hard, money is tight."[5]

In response to the suggestion that art theft became recognized only in 1970 as a major problem, the West Point librarians say that the library community, and to a lesser extent the museum community, still is not facing up to the problem that theft from their institutions poses.

There is a realization that small institutions sometimes do not realize the value of their collections and of the material in their display cases and that they could not pay for security, even if they wanted it. As a result, some are being decimated by the activities of amateur and professional thieves. Michael Moss, who is a security officer at the West Point Museum, a major tourist attraction, indicates that swords, powderhorns, buttons, and guns are a particular target for thieves. He mentions that, early on, West Point anticipated that as the ranks of collectors swelled, such thefts would become commonplace, and so steps were taken at the Point—in particular the tightening of access and security regulations— to forestall them.[6]

An advertisement in the *New York Times* of December 2, 1979 confirms Moss's opinion regarding the prevalence of thefts of artifacts:

REWARD
Large Collection of
ANTIQUE 18TH AND 19TH CENTURY
RUSSIAN AND GERMAN MILITARY
HELMETS, INSIGNIAS, AND MEDALS
ESTIMATED VALUE $100,000+
Were Stolen August 1979 From Private Collection
in Dallas, Pennsylvania. Reward Offered For
Information Leading To The Recovery of These
Sentimental and Prized Objects. Please Contact:
LUONGO ADJUSTMENT CO., INC.
116 John Street
New York, New York 10038
212/962-3322[7]

NOTES

1. Egon A. Weiss, Interview, November 2, 1979.
2. Ibid.
3. Robert E. Schnare, Interview, November 2, 1979.
4. Donald Koslow, Interview, November 2, 1979.
5. Schnare, Interview, November 2, 1979.
6. Mike Moss, Interview, November 2, 1979.
7. Luongo Adjustment Co., Advertisement, *New York Times*, December 2, 1979, p. D37.

Books constitute capital.

Thomas Jefferson

MUTILATION

Book mutilation has been with us from antiquity onward. A glaring example of this practice was carried on by Mathia Flacius, a Lutheran polemicist who, disguised as a monk, would—besides stealing volumes—use a knife to steal individual leaves.[1] Another odious practice called "grangerising" sprang up in the eighteenth century. This practice, the taking of illustrations from one book for use in another, resulted from publication by the Reverend James Granger of his *Bibliographical History of England*, which had blank pages in it that were intended for the mounting of portraits and illustrations.[2] While Granger himself seems to have been blameless, grangerizing was responsible for the destruction of countless books.

Definitions of mutilation are numerous. Indian librarian Badri Prasad says that "a book made unfit for reading purposes wholly or partially is said to be mutilated."[3] Whether mutilation is carried out with a knife or a wet thread, the result is the same. Merely tearing the work accomplishes the same purpose, but in an unpleasing manner.

The venerable Astor Library felt the effects of mutilation when Richard Boyle Davy, who had been granted alcove privileges at the behest of John Elliot Ward, was excluded from the institution for the mutilation of the two-volume *Revue de Paris*.[4] The following account appeared in the *New York Sun* on March 4, 1873:

> The facilities offered for these vandalisms are largely increased by the distrust of Mr. Straznicky, the librarian, toward his subordinates. One of the assistant librarians complains that when a mutilation or loss is discovered and

reported to Mr. Straznicky, that gentleman at once charges the offense upon the person who informs him of it, and hence very few cases of depredation are reported at all. As an instance of this he [an assistant librarian] says that last July, while looking over the *Revue de Paris*, he missed seventy pages from one volume of that important work, and thirty from another. He informed the librarian of the loss, who at once charged that he had mutilated the volume, and for some time he labored under the odium this attached to him. The real culprit was at length discovered in one of the privileged alcove readers. Mr. Straznicky was given to understand that he was suffering from an aberration of intellect, but to the assistant librarian, whose character had suffered so unjustly, he was candid enough to confess that he was drunk at the time he "made the extract." Whatever may have caused him to commit the offense he was not punished for it.[5]

An investigation disclosed that a well-meaning assistant librarian, William Corkran, had spoken to the *Sun* reporter. The result was that Corkran was informed that his services would be terminated effective April 13. A fellow librarian, A. W. Tyler, joined with Corkran in filing charges against Straznicky, whereupon Straznicky fired Tyler, too. The board declined to intervene.[6]

The problem of mutilation was cited in a recent Carnegie Council on Policy Studies report, *Fair Practices in Higher Education*, as of major proportions. The Commission noted that during 1976 in excess of one hundred articles on aspirin had been ripped from magazines.[7] A study, mentioned by the Council, was done as to the reasons why students mutilate. At Kent State, three student mutilators, two men and a woman, were interviewed by Marjorie E. Murfin and Clyde Hendrick. The thirty-minute interviews were enlightening. The woman student opined that even if she had fully understood the implication of the time and expense involved in replacement, she still would have torn out the article: "If you're going to tear it out, you'll do it anyway."[8] The two men students stated that the lack of convenient copying facilities and the lack of quality copying had angered them. They both said, however, that knowledge of the time and cost of replacement would have prevented them from tearing out the articles.[9] What is frustrating is that some people appear to feel that in tearing out what they need from a book or magazine, they are entering a silent protest against conditions at the institution which to them are unacceptable. One of the two men at Kent State might also have succumbed, despite his assertions to the contrary:

> If I'd been in the library that day I would probably have torn out the article in revenge against the university [for new regulations]. And another thing. They're raising the fee $62. I'll bet there will be a lot of mutilation in the library because of that.[10]

There was also an indication that bound magazines, to some, were considered unmutilatable, while single issues were considered fair game. The idea that a bound series of magazines is to be respected as a book, while a magazine could be taken with impunity, is interesting. Yet this is not likely to deter a student whose motivation is revenge. It is important, however, not to bear down too heavily on the notion of revenge, as this is in most cases merely a contributing cause of the problem. The problem will continue, and it is not known what to do about it. Even the presence of copy machines and the availability of additional copies of much-used items do not appear to help.

There are some steps, however, that can be taken to combat the problem. Surveys can be made to find which periodicals are most susceptible to mutilation. The University of California had part of its "hit list" published in the October 15, 1979 *Library Journal*. The periodicals which were found to be favored by mutilators were, among others: *Atlantic Monthly, Changing Times, Ebony, Esquire, Harper's, Mother Jones, Ms., Newsweek, New Times, New West, New Yorker, New York, San Francisco, Saturday Review, Science Digest, Sierra, Sports Illustrated,* and *Time.*[11]

Those who mutilate because the copy machines are either malfunctioning or not working completely can point to frustration as a cause of their behavior. One way of avoiding the problems created by malfunctioning machines is to have the copying done by staff members on staff machines. This, however, is inconvenient and expensive. The coin-operated machine is clearly necessary, and it is here to stay. The University of Toronto Library, though, is not so sure. It has staff members do the copying of materials. A survey showed that during a two-week period, February 23-March 8, 1970, five copy machines copied 21,483 pages from 1,768 items. The average number of pages per item was twelve.[12]

The use of coin-operated machines is generally dictated by staff and budgetary considerations. Little had been written about the use and choice of such coin-operated machines. The Spring, 1976 issue of *Library Resources & Technical Services* contains an article by William Saffady which deals with coin-operated copy machines. Mention is made here of the two types of coin mechanisms: those located internally (Olivetti Coinfax and SCM Coronastat 55) and those with external mechanisms (Xerox 1000 and Savin 220). Changing toner and paper on the Olivetti makes the change fund vulnerable. Consequently, care must be taken in delegating the machine's maintenance. This is not true of the SCM machine, which can be maintained without exposing the coin reserve.[13]

One other interesting consideration is the type of feed mechanism that is used in a machine—spool versus sheet. The sheets can be added at any time, while the spool should not be replaced until it is near its point of expiration.[14]

It is prudent, in light of the mutilation which occurs because of frustration with nonfunctioning copy systems, to have efficient machines and to see that they are well maintained. Perhaps if more thought were given to the choosing, operation, location, and number of copying machines, part of the mutilation problem would be solved.

NOTES

1. Lawrence S. Thompson, "Mutilatis Mutilandis," *Library Security Newsletter* 2:2 (Summer, 1978), p. 15.

2. Ibid.

3. Badri Prasad, *Problems of Misplacement, Mutilation and Theft of Books in Libraries*, p. 16.

4. Harry Miller Lydenberg, *History of the New York Public Library*, p. 56.

5. "Astor Library Troubles," *New York Sun*, March 4, 1873, p. 2.

6. Lydenberg, p. 58.

7. "Carnegie Study Finds Theft Rising in College Libraries," *Library Journal* 104 (June 1, 1979), p. 1206.

8. Marjorie E. Murfin and Clyde Hendrick, "Ripoffs Tell Their Story: Interviews With Mutilators in a University Library," *Journal of Academic Librarianship* 1:2, p. 11.

9. Ibid., p. 12.
10. Ibid., p. 9.
11. "Periodicals Hit List," *Library Journal* 104 (Oct. 15, 1979), p. 2153.
12. Robert H. Blackburn, "Photocopying in a University Library," *Scholarly Publishing* 2:1 (Oct. 1976), p. 53.
13. William Saffady, "Evaluating Coin-Operated Copying Equipment for Library Application," *Library Resources & Technical Services* 20:2 (Spring 1976), p. 118.
14. Ibid., p. 119.

Property is theft.

Pierre-Joseph Proudhon

THE VALUE OF VALUES

There are times when something considered to be of no value may in fact be valuable. Circumstances can make the most ephemeral of items of importance to collectors. The recent sale of Frederick E. Church's "Icebergs" for $2.3 million caused an individual to write the following letter to the *New York Times*:

> Relative to the $2.3 million paid for Frederick E. Church's painting "Icebergs," I have before me a letter dated May 26, 1888, from a chemical supply company agreeing that farmer Church should have been charged the wholesale price of 2.3 cents instead of the retail price of 2.5 cents a pound for several hundred pounds of nitrate of soda, and that they were therefore crediting his account with 40 cents.[1]

Surely, once this item was seen there would be people who would want the letter, despite the fact that it was not written by Church. Many persons must be combing their attics in the hope of finding such items.

The Church work itself was, of course, greatly valuable. This work was "lost" for many years; and one can only speculate as to the number of lost masterworks that await rediscovey. Grace Glueck claims that a lost da Vinci, over which Vasari has painted a fresco, has been found. This was da Vinci's 1505 work, "The Battle of Anghiari."[2] It is expected that this event will spur the finding of lost paintings by other masters.

There are few sensations to equal the thrill of unearthing a genuine treasure. Occasionally, however, the pleasure can be spoiled. According to Robert Schnare, important works can be uncovered in the recesses of almost any library, but in publicizing the finding, the risk is run of having the item "ripped off."[3]

Thieves are discriminating. Egon A. Weiss of the U.S. Military Academy Library tells the story of the library which found that a New York City directory (which weighs about forty pounds) had been stolen. The library replaced the stolen volume with a newer edition; one week later the new edition was gone, but the old one was returned to take its place (the culprit evidently had a conscience, even if it did not function flawlessly).[4]

Apparently nothing is sacred, not even the cap of Sigmund Freud. The Freud Museum in Vienna, which claims among its treasures the walking stick, handbag, and umbrella of Sigmund Freud, found that thieves had been at work. A replacement cap was found to have been substituted for the original. The label inside the cap was what led museum authorities to realize that a theft had occurred. It was decided to have graphologists check the visitors book. Yet visitors are not required to sign the book, and it is doubtful, of course, that this would have helped solve the crime, even if the thief had been obliging enough to have left his or her signature behind. Freud's cap was valued at 100,000 Austrian Schillings, or $7,000.[5]

A bizarre case concerns the skull of the composer Haydn. This was acquired by two men who bribed a gravedigger. They displayed their treasure as follows: "They put it in a black lacquer box decorated with a golden lyre, with a little window through which they could peek at the skull resting on a white satin cushion."[6]

Years later, when Prince Milos Eszterhazy had Haydn's remains exhumed in preparation for reburial in a splendid mausoleum, the head was found to be missing. The prince offered a bribe to the skull's owners, who gave the prince a skull, but it was not that of Haydn. Earlier, the prince had had the house of one of the men, a certain Rosenbaum, searched. Nothing was found. Rosenbaum's wife had feigned illness, lying on a mattress into which the skull was sewn. Ultimately, the skull went the Musical Society in Vienna as a deathbed bequest of Rosenbaum.[7]

Many times thieves will know collections they prey upon as well as or better than curators. One ploy used by thieves is to request only materials that belong in portions of collections which are either unnumbered or unprocessed.[8] This makes detection almost impossible, unless the thief attempts to dispose of the stolen items. Discretion in the use of unprotected materials is always advisable. It is usually true that valuables remain safe if their existence is unknown.

NOTES

1. Howard Frisch, Letter to the Editor, *New York Times*, Nov. 2, 1979, p. A22.

2. Grace Glueck, "Lost Da Vinci Mural Believed Discovered," *New York Times*, Nov. 2, 1979, p. 1.

3. Robert Schnare, Interview, Nov. 2, 1979.

4. Egon A. Weiss, Interview, Nov. 2, 1979.

5. Emery Kelen, "Hats Off to Daring Thief of Herr Freud's Cap," *U.N. Observor and International Reporter* II:II (Dec. 1979), p. 6.

6. Ibid.

7. Ibid.

8. Schnare, Nov. 2, 1979.

*A fraud is not perfect unless it be
practiced on clever persons.*

Arab Proverb

THE FORGER'S CONSIDERATIONS

The subject of forgeries may seem to be the stuff of best-selling movies. Forgeries of both documents and paintings have on occasion fooled the greatest authorities, and tales of such forgeries abound.

Archival materials lend themselves quite readily to forgery. According to Cheryl A. Price,

> An archive may be more exposed to forgeries than a museum in that when materials are presented to it, the materials are often measured in cubic feet of documents. Thus, it is difficult to make the minute examination that a curator might make before a purchase.[1]

The sophisticated forger will do whatever is needed to make his or her forgery appear genuine. The problem of dating ink and paper calls for specialists. Paper was, prior to the twentieth century, made carefully and in small quantities. The tracing of the authenticity of the paper of earlier documents is thus scientifically possible. The paper of documents of more recent vintage can be identified by type, design, watermark, and other such matters. The Alger Hiss case, in which a certain typewriter was shown to have been used in writing a particular series of letters, was a milestone in the authentication of such evidence. Another point of identification, in the case of government documents, is an ink stamp impression found on the paper. This is customarily used in the case of a classified document.

Perhaps the most readily discernable manner of detecting a

forgery is to examine the ink. The ink for ball-point pens, for instance, differs from the thinner inks used in fountain pens. Wilson R. Harrison writes that although ball point pens began to be used in the mid 1940s, the ink used then was found unsuitable, and a different type was substituted in the 1950s.[2]

The glue used on envelope flaps can provide a clue to forgeries. Cheryl A. Price mentions that only since World War II have synthetic resins been used in such glues or adhesives.[3] Thus, the use of synthetic adhesives on an envelope said to be from the 1920s would indicated that something was wrong.

The Society of American Archivists has not yet reached the point of considering the authentication and certification of documents as an area requiring licensing. In Britain, on the other hand, three years are required to train a document examiner.[4] The area is clearly a highly specialized one, and it is believed that eventually the area will be recognized everywhere for what it is.

There are those professional dealers and collectors who can identify an original and spot a forgery with ease. Charles Hamilton tells how he was shown one word on a piece of paper by a railroad porter. He successfully identified the paper as having been written by Robert Frost and purchased it from its amazed owner.[5]

An enterprising forger, Robert Spring, made his living personalizing George Washington letters for members of old-line Philadelphia families. Although these forgeries are now valued as curiosities, some no doubt continue to be thought of as genuine Washington authographs. Hamilton says: "Even today the field of Revolutionary War collecting is still booby-trappd with Spring's forgeries..."[6]

There are motives other than monetary gain for the use of forgery. There have been concentrated efforts by some forgers to get some of their forgeries enrolled in series of documents held by archives.[7] Who would bother to question one letter which is part of countless cubic feet of documents? Reasons for such behavior are not hard to ascertain. For instance, a person might attempt to place a forgery in an archive as a means of supporting a favored historical notion that lacks documentation.

In addition, the idea of a group of politicians planting such a document to obscure or confuse actual happenings is not beyond the realm of possibility. One of the alleged duties of E. Howard

Hunt, author and ex-CIA operative, was to counterfeit cables which were said to have originated in Saigon. A forgery of this sort would be almost certainly undetectable.

NOTES

1. Cheryl A. Price, "Document Examination in American Archives," *Special Libraries* 68:9, p. 301.

2. Wilson R. Harrison, "Dating Documents," *Criminal Law Review* 3:387 (June 1956), p. 387.

3. Price, p. 303.

4. Ibid., p. 304.

5. Charles Hamilton, *The Book of Autographs*, p. 19.

6. Charles Hamilton, *Scribblers and Scoundrels*, p. 166.

7. Price, p. 301.

Take all your savings and buy some good stock
and hold it till it goes up and then sell it.
If it doesn't go up, don't buy it.

Will Rogers, October 1, 1929

THE INVESTMENT FALLACY

Rare books and manuscripts have been touted as good investments and as a hedge against inflation. It is because of such pronouncements that many rare books and manuscripts have been stolen. Yet the idea that a manuscript will be a good investment per se is spurious.

Even assuming that one has the necessary expertise—which is a major assumption—rare books and manuscripts are not necessarily prudent investments. Robert Schnare, Special Collections Librarian at West Point, comments: "If you know what you're doing, maybe. In most cases, it's not a good investment because people don't really know what they're doing."[1]

Perhaps if the public were disabused as to the monetary value of rare books and manuscripts and visions of soaring profits, the archival library world could rest more securely than it does. Whenever a report of a major sale of materials appears, it is followed almost invariably by a series of thefts of like material.

If one knows when and what to buy and when to sell, he or she stands to make a reasonable profit, but the uncertainties of the business are rife. Who could have known that Frost's *A Boy's Will* or Faulkner's *Marble Fawn* would one day be immensely valuable? The notion that such investments are "sure things," however, can lead to problems and is certainly as dangerous—and perhaps more so—to the neophyte investor in this field as it is to those with a specialized knowledge of the field: collectors, librarians, archivists, and dealers.

NOTES

1. Robert Schnare, Interview, Nov. 2, 1979.

*Laws exist in vain for those who have not the
courage and the means to defend them.*

Thomas Macaulay

THE FBI

Thefts of library and archival material fall within the jurisdiction of the FBI in cases in which there has been interstate transport of items valued in excess of $5,000 (Sections 2314 and 2315 Title 18 U.S. Code). The Bureau may also become involved if the theft utilizes radio or television facilities (fraud by wire violations Section 1343 Title 18 U.S. Code.). The FBI has jurisdiction likewise under the Theft of Government Property Statute if the materials stolen are the property of the U.S. Government (Section 661 Title 18 U.S. Code). Finally, if unlawful flight to avoid prosecution takes place, the FBI may enter a case.[1]

FBI Agent Thomas McShane states that there is a twelve-man major theft squad in New York City from which men are assigned to work on cases. There is no "hot list" of art or books or manuscripts.[2]

It turns out that in practice, at least in New York, the FBI declines to handle cases in which the value of the stolen property is less than $50,000.[3] Exceptions would occur in cases involving massive publicity or in which the presence of the FBI is requested by local authorities.

NOTES

1. William J. Riley, "Library Security and the Federal Bureau of Investigation," *College and Research Libraries* 38:2, p. 106.

2. Thomas McShane, Telephone interview, May 7, 1979.

3. Anonymous source.

To build is to be robbed.

Samuel Johnson, 1759

DESIGN OF BUILDINGS

Buildings not designed with security in mind may be marvels of art and architecture, but if they are insecure, they lack an essential quality of the good public building. Ada Louise Huxtable's assessment of the Kennedy Library in the *New York Times* underscores this problem:

> What has happened, of course, is that the union of library and museum has unexpectedly gone askew; it has turned into a Catch-22 shotgun marriage. The museum function has expanded to a point where it has taken over more and more overtly from the archives. The result is an odd architectural couple with the library serving as an excuse for the museum.[1]

The idea of a library designed for scholarly research and that of "the biggest draw since Disneyland"[2] are not compatible. The supposition is that security will be devoted to the museum quarters of the facility, especially as this is concerned with crowd steering and overall control. Huxtable says rightly that "scholars and museum-goers, like oil and water, will not mix."[3] It is clear that this building is something of a security expert's nightmare. One can hope that the safeguarding of the archives will not be subordinated too greatly to the need for security in the museum, but there is a question that this is in fact what is happening. Huxtable certainly has grave doubts: "It is clearer than ever that the archives are misplaced as part of the museum: the marriage of convenience has turned into an awkward and costly relationship."[4]

Such misuse of space in planning is not only confined to libraries and museums. New York theaters have been designed without dressing rooms. And strange to relate, these are recent buildings, not those built at a time when actors' needs were little more than afterthought.

One hears of a building which was designed with large windows of lexan, a pliable material which cannot be shattered. The person wishing to enter or leave merely bends the panes in the doorway so that they slip from their moorings. The idea may have had merit. Unfortunately, however, burglaries were so numerous that steel plates had to be welded over the entire front of the building. The result was a building to which entrance became well-nigh impossible. Opting for such an "open" design obviously has disadvantages.

Security provisions are an expensive afterthought. The cost of altering buildings to repair security deficiencies is generally huge. Security must be given considerable priority in the design of libraries and archival buildings. Clearly, this was not done in the case of the Kennedy Library. Museum officials speak of processing 6,000 visitors a day.[5] While these people are being processed, one can wonder about the arrangements that hold for people who wish to use the library. The answer is not encouraging:

> The archives are there but they are more or less tucked into the ceiling. The Presidential and other papers are literally housed in two tightly compressed floors at the very top of the structure with audio-visual material in a kind of ceiling plenum of the main ceremonial hall.[6]

The architecture of a building can be a boon or bane to a potential thief, mugger, purse snatcher, or library materials thief. Security consultant Charles F. Hemphill, Jr., writes:

> It is also suggested that the architect eliminate hidden recesses, abutments, projections, or other building features that would allow concealment of intruders. Experience shows that in most instances two police officers in one patrol car can adequately cover the exterior of a building from opposite corners. But the effectiveness of this coverage can be canceled out by architectural features that allow an outsider to hide on the premises. If building walls are painted a light color, it

is usually easier to spot the outline of an intruder on the premises at night.[7]

Library and museum buildings will, as insurance companies begin to take more interest in the security features of buildings, become places whose design reflects some input from a security point of view. It should be remembered that fire regulation must be considered in conjunction with security considerations. Often enough it happens that security requires the locking of an exit that from a fire safety perspective ought to remain unlocked. Trade-offs occur, and these must be adjudged on their merits. The fact that security considerations must be given their due in the overall design of a building will save costly renovations after the building is completed. This notion, it is hoped, will eventually work its way into the psyche of trustees, officials, and members of planning boards.

It is wrong, of course, to suppose that archival materials are stolen only during the hours that the facility is open. Timothy Walch has warned: "Even though break-ins do not commonly occur in archival repositories, they do happen on occasion."[8]

The subject of security systems other than those for book theft detection purposes was treated in *Library Technology Reports*, March 1977, in an article whch began; "While book theft is a very important issue in library security many libraries are in need of other security systems, especially to prevent and detect vandalism which occurs during the hours when the library is closed."[9] The article deals with three major security considerations: point protection, perimeter protection, and space protection. Presented in question-and-answer format, it introduces the many other security systems that can be useful to libraries. The systems are listed according to the three categories, and the names and addresses of manufacturers are given.

It is advisable, and probably necessary, to seek out the advice of a good security consultant during the planning stages of a new building. To wait longer than this is, as suggested, to court disaster.

Descriptions of security systems for new buildings appear in such books as Gerald Shirar's *Protecting Works of Art*, or Charles F. Hemphill's *Modern Security Methods*. Timothy Walch's *Archives and Manuscripts Security* provides a good introduction to the subject. The other books are more technically oriented, however, and intended specifically for the use of the security professional.

The details of security operation are divulged on a "need to know" basis. As a precaution, what systems are in use is generally a carefully guarded secret. Such information, in naive or wrong hands, could, of course, create grave damage.

Surveillance systems will be discussed in a separate chapter. These systems will be discussed from the standpoint of cost versus potential benefit. There are heat-sensitive systems, motion-sensitive systems, and weight-sensitive systems, to name but a few types. The choosing of such a system is a complicated matter, one in which the expertise of the security consultant should be sought.

Locks, safes, and vaults are also in the purview of the specialist. The books mentioned previously deal in some depth with these. All that will be said here is that locks and keys must be carefully controlled and that the reputation of the locksmiths one uses must be irreproachable.

Thus, security involves the help of electricians, plumbers, locksmiths, builders, and a myriad of related professionals. The keynote is cooperation between these people and the institution. Without it, security is unattainable.

NOTES

1. Ada Louise Huxtable, "The Museum Upstages the Library," *New York Times*, Oct. 28, 1979, p. 31D.
2. Ibid.
3. Ibid., p. 39D.
4. Ibid.
5. Ibid., p. 31D.
6. Ibid., p. 39D.
7. Charles F. Hemphill, Jr., *Modern Security Methods*, p. 17.
8. Timothy Walch, *Archives and Manuscripts Security*, p. 10.
9. "Questions and Answers," *Library Technology Reports* 13:123 (March 1977), p. 123.

They also serve who stand and wait.

Milton

GUARDS

The guard is often required to do more than just guard the facility and its contents. Charles F. Hemphill, Jr., author of *Modern Security Methods*, defines the overall guard function:

> Used in other functions, a guard may control access, escort visitors within the facility, and regulate compliance with company rules. The guard may also be an ambassador of company goodwill, furnishing information, assisting visitors, and regulating foot traffic and vehicles. If performing public relations duties, the guard may be outfitted in a blazer and slacks rather than in a conventional uniform.[1]

Thus, the guard must be an employee of high caliber. He must be knowedgeable and courteous. Frank J. De Rosa, head of security at the Brooklyn Public Library, feels that a good security person is able to deal with intricate public relations situations, while at the same time maintaining the confidence and goodwill of all concerned.

The qualifications of persons hired as guards are sometimes insufficient to allow them to perform their function properly. Gerald Shirar of the American Society of Industrial Security warns:

> A museum is ill-advised to continue to invest in a force made up of those physically incapable of meeting the potential demands of the job. Loyalty to the museum and its collection is insufficient. The job of guarding a museum requires a modern approach, employing techniques proven in other security situations.[2]

91

The potential demands of the job may well require the ability to run up or down stairs or merely a sufficient presence, either mental or physical, to deal successfully with difficult situations. "Security is handling people and having a good presence," says Frank De Rosa.[3] An air of self-assurance is needed, a confidence born of knowledge and maturity. Bravado and intimidation are no part of the makeup of the guard.

Guards should not be armed. The guards at the Brooklyn Public Library do not even carry clubs. Again, this emphasizes the idea that the guard should be able to deal with a situation peaceably. Talk is always preferable to force. Circumstances that make necessary the presence of armed guards call for highly trained persons from a firm with the highest reputation.

The proliferation of "rent a cop" firms which have placed untrained and often club-wielding individuals in stores here and there has given a bad image to all guard services. The professional services which have been in operation and are of proven quality (Pinkerton, Burns, Wackenhut, to name but a few) provide businesses and agencies with superb protection. The guards they supply are bonded; they are highly trained and motivated persons who can function at various levels in any organization. The choice of an in-house guard sevice or the hiring of a professional guard force from one of these major firms was considered by Pat Schindler: "Some security directors feel that having guards directly on their own payroll gives them better control and more responsiveness from the people. Others feel that this restricts them in their ability to remove personnel that they feel are marginal or undesirable."[4]

The deportment of the guards must be above reproach. Courtesy and respect are essential in the carrying out of the guard's duties. Pat Schindler comments:

> A discourteous clerk is one thing and although undesirable, is more readily accepted than a remark from a discourteous security guard. An elementary knowledge of proper image projection [is necessary] and a thorough knowledge of the library, its layout and other vital information such as hours, policies, etc.[5]

The maintenance of a high degree of self-respect in the guard force is essential. Schindler mentions four duties which guards should not be expected to perform:

1. Janitorial duties.
2. Book shelving.
3. Disciplining employees who violate rules.
4. Demeaning duties that lower the esteem of the guards in the eyes of employees and visitors.[6]

It is possible that having on the premises a person in a uniform may create problems itself. There are situations into which no guard will intrude. Suits for false arrest do occur, and so it is essential that guards have a knowledge of the law and the presence of mind to recognize entrapment for what it is. Guards must also be confident that their superiors will back them in any actions they take in pursuit of duty.

Much is expected of guards. What must also be considered is the responsibility of the institution toward its guards. Regarding the responsibilities of a museum to its guards-attendants, Georges Sportouch writes:

> The attendant or security guard should occupy a worthy position and be conscience of holding a post of responsibility. He should always be informed of what is being done, of what practical preparations are being made in the museum (and, if possible, he should play a part in setting up an exhibition for the security of which he will be responsible); this approach is likely to make him more interested in his work and in what the museum is doing.[7]

The security force under the Brooklyn Public Library's security chief Frank J. De Rosa is without question a truly professional corps of men and women. The average age of its members is forty. Their salary average is $12,000.[8] Their counterparts at the New York Public Library have an $8,000 starting salary. Members of the Brooklyn Public Library's security force are carefully screened before they are hired, and they are trained, once they are on the force, with equal care. Security is their only function. An indication of the quality of the guard force at this institution is evidenced in the fact that De Rosa's second in command was promoted from the ranks of his own security force.

At the New York Public Library the guards are members of the building and maintenance staff. Their official designation is Library Attendant Guard. These uniformed guards are supervised by senior investigators, who wear blue shirts with library insignia on their collars. The guards are the library's first line of security; among their duties they must examine briefcases and other items before people leave the building by one of the two public exists. The guards stationed at the entrance to the two main reading rooms check each person as he or she enters or leaves. I have observed the guards and found them to be courteous but thorough in the performance of their duties. Some patrons, usually first-time users, are surprised at the stringency of security. The pleasant, courteous professionalism of the guards, both male and female, however, is reassuring.

The question arises as to whether guards should wear uniforms. Most security experts feel that the uniform should be worn, as the uniform alone offers a deterrent effect. De Rosa indicates that 50 percent of the effectiveness of deterrence is in the visible effect created.[9] Further, the uniform, if it is immaculate and pressed, gives the guard a sense of pride and well-being. Blazers and slacks may be substituted if a uniform is not acceptable in some situations.

Observing people and spotting those who are potential threats or troublemakers is of great importance in the guard-security function. A new problem is now presenting itself, and this is the threat of ideological vandalism. Incidents such as that in which a deranged young man slashed Rembrandt's "Nightwatch" and the sculptor who attacked Michelangelo's "Pieta" with a hammer illustrate this trend.

Security people indicate that ideological damage to works of art is an ever present threat. The reasons behind such actions of destruction are many. Guy Rosolato offers a suggestion as to why works of art are attacked:

> It is significant that art should be the first to suffer from these chaotic acts. Its purpose, as Freud has shown, is to make use of fantasies which are inadmissible but which are sufficiently well concealed by the interest the onlooker takes in the organization of forms. But a certain kind of paranoid sensibility establishes direct contact with the

underlying fantasy. The aesthetic integument with its easy play of ambiguities, melts away. What is more, the interpretation becomes enormously projective.[10]

This being the case, the guard force must be ever alert. Thus, the skill level, motivation, and capability of the guards must be high. Visitors are screened and summed up as trustworthy or not from the very moment they enter a great library or museum. The person who seems to be paying too much attention to a particular piece will almost certainly be placed under radio and television surveillance. Silent alerts are sometimes used to bring special squads to various floors. These squads do nothing but observe. All this goes on without the knowledge or understanding of the general public.

The necessity for close contact between security departments and local agencies is very great. Small groups within the public often invade public buildings. Not the least of these is the group made up of "crazies." The behavior of such people can be destructive but is usually no worse than disturbing to others. In any event, such persons and their habits become known to security officers who keep a wary eye out for prospective outbreaks. The rule is that it is better to have surveillance than to risk an untoward incident. The very fact that nothing happens indicates that the security force is functioning properly.

The security system always aims for a zero rate of incidents. Although the role of prevention is stressed in security work, security is not a dull occupation. The battle of wits continues uninterruptedly. Every stranger is measured against a mental scale which can sense a troublemaker, a thief casing a display, or a problem that requires the alerting of people elsewhere.

De Rosa indicates that buildings are not built with security in mind. The result is that problems are created which must be dealt with at greater expense later.[11] Many buildings have had their security offices added as an afterthought. Sometimes these are relegated to lesser-traveled parts of the building or are tucked away in a corner. Whether or not this is a good thing remains a subject of debate. While some security directors like to have their offices located conspicuously in the center of things, others prefer an obscure location, one that is not even indicated on the guide maps of their building.

Some people lamentably regard the security operation as a necessary evil about which they want to know little. If these people were aware of the crimes foiled and the other unpleasantnesses averted through the diligence of their security agents, their opinion would change drastically. Good security service is largely invisible, but no less useful for its secretiveness.

In view of the limitations that hamper the guards at the New York Public Library, it is understandable that Walter Zervas of the New York Public Library would confide to *Time*: "If ever there was a treasure house that's going to wrack and ruin, this is it."[12] The guards and security seem to have no backing, even when someone is apprehended for crimes more serious than theft of library materials. Security Officer Sivert Olenius comments upon the apathy of the public: "We can't do a thing unless the [injured] person presses charges."[13] This, in and of itself, is a frustrating situation.

The problem is that institutions like the New York Public Library and the Brooklyn Public Library are public institutions—some might say too public. The unsavoriness of Bryant Park, which abuts on the New York Public Library at 42nd Street, and the vicious character of West 42nd Street beyond have made matters worse. The credo of the library force has been to serve the public well. The nature of the public in the area of the library, however, appears to be changing for the worse.

The location of an institution determines in large measure the sort of public it attracts. The locations of the New York Public Library and the Brooklyn Public Library (Grand Army Plaza) create problems for these institutions. The location of the new Kennedy Library, which was to have been in congested Cambridge but was moved instead to Columbia Point, has seemingly reduced concerns over disruptive patrons and theft.

NOTES

1. Charles Hemphill, Jr., *Modern Security Methods*, p. 8.
2. Gerald Shirar, *Protecting Works of Art*, p. 59.
3. Frank J. De Rosa, Interview, Aug. 27, 1979.
4. Pat Schindler, "The Use of Security Guards in Libraries," *Library Security Newsletter* 2:2 (Summer 1978), p. 5.
5. Ibid., p. 3.
6. Ibid.

7. Georges Sportouch, "Museum Attendants." In *Protecting Works of Art,* Gerald Shirar, comp., p. 69.

8. De Rosa, Interview, Aug. 27, 1979.

9. Ibid.

10. Guy Rosolato, "Psychoanalytic Notes on the Theft and Defacement of Works of Art." In *Protecting Works of Art,* p. 25.

11. De Rosa, Interview, Aug. 27, 1979.

12. Walter Zervas, quoted in David Aikman's "Reading Between the Lions," *Time* 114 (Oct. 8, 1979), p. 20.

13. Sivert Olenius, quoted in "Reading Between the Lions," p. 20.

No man is above the law and no man is below it nor do we ask any man's permission when we require him to obey it.

Theodore Roosevelt

THE SECURITY FORCE AS PEACE OFFICERS

Members of security forces can receive appointments as peace officers. For instance, Section 434 A-7.0 of the New York City Administratve Code allows the Police Commissioner of that city to appoint security officers as special patrolmen. These persons have peace officer status during the exercise of their official duties. The peace officer has the power to arrest, without a warrant, under New York State Criminal procedure Law Section 140:25 as follows:

1. A peace officer other than a police officer, *acting pursuant to his special duties*, may arrest a person for:

    a. Any *offense*, when he has reasonable cause to believe that such person has committed such offense in his presence; and

    b. A *crime*, when he has reasonable cause to believe that such person has committed such crime, whether in his presence or otherwise.

2. A peace officer other than a police officer may act "pursuant to his special duties" in making an arrest only when the arrest is for:

    a. An *offense* defined by a statute which such peace offficer, by reason of the specialized nature of his particular employment or by express provision of law, is required or authorized to enforce; or

    b. An *offense* committed or reasonably believed by him to have been committed in such manner or place as to render

98

arrest of the offender by such peace officer under the particular circumstances an integral part of his specialized duties.

Security officers who have not been deputized as Special Patrolman have the same arrest powers as private persons...[1]

Different states have different regulations. It is essential that members of the security force understand the limitations of their peace officer status. Failure of such understanding could well embroil the facility in a costly and embarrassing lawsuit for false arrest, unlawful search or seizure, kidnapping, or a related charge.

It is a rare enough occasion on which a security officer with such status will use his or her special authority. The security staff must be firmly confident that their superiors will back them in their decisions. The supervisor, on the other hand, must have faith in the ability of the security force to use their powers of arrest with discrimination.

NOTES

1. Brooklyn Public Library Security Department Training Memo No. 1, March 21, 1979, p. 1.

*It is far pleasanter to sit comfortably in the shade
rubbing red pepper into a poor devil's eyes than to
go about in the sun hunting up evidence.*

Sir James Stephens

SURVEILLANCE

What to observe and how to observe are matters of great importance to security officers. There are two basic types of surveillance:

1. Physical surveillance: The actual observation of other persons, activities, or places, by the human eye and the proper recording of this information.
2. Technical surveillance: The employment of technical equipment such as cameras, radios, electronic monitoring equipment, etc., for the purpose of preserving observations made during the surveillance, etc. Usually, basic elements of physical surveillance will be contained in this type of operation.[1]

Let us assume that a patron, who is suspected of concealing library materials on his or her person, is being watched. In this instance, "moving surveillance" is generally required. Principles of this type of surveillance might include the following:

1. Keep the subject (or location) under observation at all times regardless of whether you are "made" (identified as a surveillance agent).
2. Conduct a discreet surveillance and break off (discontinue) rather than be "made."
3. Keep the subject or location under observation at all times and do not get "made."[2]

When to observe one or another of these principles depends upon prevailing circumstances.

Examples of what security officers look for are not hard to ascertain. For instance, if a person is observed placing pictures or other materials in piles, the security officer's curiosity is aroused. It could be that such activity is innocent. On the other hand, the sorting may be a prelude to a theft, as even thieves have been known to be choosy.[3]

Libraries and other institutions have a legal right to place a surveillance on their employees or to "tail" trucks or other library vehicles driven by library employees.[4] And while such behavior may seem reprehensible, nevertheless it must occasionally be allowed. White-collar crime is on the increase, and stern measures are needed to bring it in check.

Technical surveillance is most often carried out through use of closed-circuit television cameras. Dummy television cameras are sometimes used, as these are a surprisingly effective deterrent. De Rosa points out that one panning and zoom lens camera can cost as much as three conventional closed-circuit cameras.[5] The dummy camera, which costs very little, then, has a place in security work.

According to Albert J. Grossman, the Cleveland Museum not only uses cameras, but has also installed microphones with the cameras, so that sound is available along with the picture.[6] The sound is thought to be especially helpful at night when the museum is closed, as it gives notice of disturbances the camera is unable to detect.

The placement of a monitoring station should be such that the public can see that the cameras are functioning. De Rosa suggests that a control center placed at the entrance to the facility has a high deterrent value.[7] Furthermore, if security is to be promoted, the monitor must be manned at all times, and there must be an effective communications network so that immediate contact can be made with all necessary security personnel.

The cost of such systems must be weighed against their potential value. Not all libraries can afford television protection; television can be prohibitively expensive when buildings are large and the spaces in them full of obstructions, but for those that can afford it, it provides an excellent form of protection.

The more exotic types of surveillance are not something in which libraries and museums would, as a rule, be interested. One type of monitoring which is legal is the recording of telephone conversations. No longer is the recording beep necessary if one of the parties is recording the conversation.[8] What is illegal is wire-tapping which is "implemented without the consent of any of the parties to the conversation."[9] The penalities are severe. Such activities can be carried on only by duly authorized law enforcement agencies, and these agencies must have a court order to allow each specific tap.

A form of surveillance that may once have been legal is now in violation of the law. Certain Las Vegas casinos had installed and were using microphones at craps and baccarat tables for the ostensible purpose of "preventing dealers from pressuring for tips." One can well imagine that other reasons existed for the use of these microphones, such as the spotting of card counters and suspicious activities in general, on the part of both patrons and casino staff. The Nevada Attorney General's office ruled on December 23, 1980 that the placement of such microphones at gaming tables "for the purpose of monitoring conversations" was a violation of "both state and federal laws."[10] Museums, libraries, and other facilities with such monitoring devices will watch the follow-up of this decision with interest.

Any sort of photographic surveillance requires the use of special equipment by highly trained professionals. Such operations are not within the budgetary reach of most libraries; nor are they necessary. A snapshot taken with a small camera using fast film is usually acceptable if a photo of a particular person is required. The legality of such an operation is, however, open to interpretation.

Generally, the simpler the surveillance, the better it is. An alert staff which is trained to notice the telltale signs that something is amiss can notify the security department so that necessary measures can be enacted.

NOTES

1. American Society for Industrial Security, *A Guide to Security Investigations*, p. 197.

2. Ibid., p. 98.

3. Anonymous interview.

4. Charles F. Hemphill, Jr., *Modern Security Methods*, p. 181.

5. Frank De Rosa, Interview, Aug. 27, 1979.

6. Albert J. Grossman, "Television-Museum Watchdog." In *Protecting Works of Art*, Gerald Shirar, comp., p. 189.

7. De Rosa, Interview, Aug. 27, 1979.

8. Steven Brill, "Muscled By The F.B.I.," *Esquire* 90:8 (Oct. 10, 1978), p. 18.

9. ASIS, *A Guide to Industrial Security*, p. 100.

10. "Casinos' Microphones Ruled Illegal in Nevada," *New York Times*, Dec. 24, 1980, p. B4.

What is come by dishonesty vanished in profligacy.

Cicero

EMPLOYEE DISHONESTY

Employee dishonesty is a subject about which nobody likes to talk. Until recently, the subject of white-collar crime was hardly ever broached, even though this form of crime costs employers losses in the billions of dollars every year. The advent of computer crimes, however, has brought about a change. White-collar crime is now the subject of headlines. If it were once possible for dishonest employees to milk employers of thousands of dollars, the amount has now grown, with the computer's help, into the hundreds of thousands.

In a story in the *New York Times* on July 10, 1979, Selwyn Rabb tells how an unnamed manager of the two retail bookshops of the New York Public Library was dismissed after an audit indicated that $82,000 had been paid by this library for nonexistent supplies.[1] The scheme did not represent a simple theft, but was rather one that required a complex knowledge of library accounting procedures. David J. Bauer, one New York Public Library Vice President, was quoted as having said: "We believe that he created fictitious companies and had payments made to them which he apparently collected for himself."[2] The manager had been at his $21,000 post for about fifteen years and had run two shops with a combined yearly budget of $225,000.

The man was not named because, among other reasons, the matter was being turned over to the D.A.'s office for possible prosecution. It was the tagline to the story which gave an idea of what would happen: "Mr. Bauer said the $82,000 loss was expected to be recovered through insurance."[3]

This loss is not something for which security could be held responsible. Supposedly, auditing and accounting deficiencies played a part in the matter, but whether or not this was actually so is uncertain. The closing of the Lincoln Center shop was deemed to be unrelated to the incident involving the $82,000. The *Times* indicated that it had learned about the story through independent means. The manager's reaction to the charges was not given: "Officials at the Library also refused to say what the manager's response had been when he was confronted with the charge that the funds had been misallocated."[4] Bauer is quoted as saying: "He was a nice fellow you would never think would do anything wrong."[5]

Long-term employees are understandably exempt from the usual interrogations that take place when a white-collar crime is being unearthed. Sadly, however, even these employees sometimes turn out not to be incorruptible. As in mystery novels, so in real life—the people who are not suspected are often the guilty ones.

The suggestion continues to be heard that the polygraph test be used to determine the honesty or lack of honesty of employees. However, the opposition of unions, professional organizations, and civil liberties groups to the idea, as well as a general distaste for it, makes it clear that this is not the way out. The legal status of the polygraph varies from state to state.

These and other matters relating to the polygraph are discussed in a book by Stanley Abrams, *A Polygraph Handbook for Attorneys*. According to Abrams, the polygraph is generally thought of as a device for use solely in criminal cases. He continues: "This is rather unfortunate considering its great worth in civil cases."[6]

There are, of course, ways and means of beating the polygraph. A thorough discussion of these can be found in John Marks's *The Search for the Manchurian Candidate: The CIA and Mind Control.*[7] Likewise, many books written by former intelligence officers address themselves to this matter, as do a goodly number of articles with the Kennedy assassination theories.

Among the security people with whom I talked, opinion on the use and potential of the polygraph was divided. One source told me that the machine could serve as a useful tool in learning more about an employee. He suggested that its use was not always harmful. It could, for instance, provide a reason for hiring somebody who had been rated in more usual tests as marginal.[8]

Nevertheless, the fact that the machine is only as good as its operator—the person establishing the inquiry conditions and interpreting the results—combined with the possibility of its being beaten, makes the instrument in the view of many of dubious general value.

Thieves can and will steal anything of value. There are many items in a library which the thief might look upon as fair game. The rugs on the floor or walls of certain sumptuous rooms have attracted the attention of thieves. The *New York Times* reported the following on September 2, 1979: "Thieves who were stealing the rugs out from under people—well almost—were reported operating last April in Boston. They were described as a super specialized breed of burglar whose target was strictly oriental rugs."[9]

Rugs are not all that has been stolen. Yale University was embarrassed to report that the President's Collar, a gold and silver bejeweled necklace valued at $100,000 was missing as of September 29, 1979. The details of this crime were startlingly simple. The vault box was found to be empty when someone went to retrieve the collar for a ceremony. The vault, it transpired, was customarily left unlocked during the day and only locked at night. The vault lock combination was known to several office workers.[10]

Items which one would not consider worth stealing are often enough the very things that go missing.

In general problems of security in libraries and the ease with which these and similar institutions fall prey to thieves have caused insurance companies to scrutinize policies and conditions of continuing coverage. The Public Library of Rockport, Maine was given an Eastman Johnson painting, "Sugaring Off At The Camp," in 1953. The library could not provide proper security for the work or even afford insurance for it, as its annual budget was $9,000, and so was forced to sell it. The amount realized was $320,000.[11]

Many libraries and public buildings have paintings and other objects the value of which is occasionally not fully comprehended. A surge of interest in a particular author, for instance, can bring with it a rash of thefts of the works of that author. Years ago, such a situation overtook library holdings of the works of H. P. Lovecraft. And more recently, Winslow Homer covers and prints have disappeared in large numbers from libraries in many parts of the country.

Theft can be engaged in for reasons other than monetary gain. Many libraries have found that their collections of works on Ethiopia have suffered through theft and mutilation. A project begun in 1965 in Ethiopia by the Reverend Godfrey Diekmann, a Benedictine Monk and Professor of Early Church History at St. John's University in New York City, to microfilm and fully catalog such materials, especially ancient manuscripts, called attention to the fact that "the contents of irreplaceable documents do succumb to the ravages of natural or military disasters and the avarice of unscrupulous scholars."[12]

There are those who steal or mutilate books so that texts with more acceptable versions will be placed on the shelves. This charge has frequently been leveled against religious groups whose beliefs have changed over the years. Another group of people, who act against that which they consider obscene, insert printed cards which tell the reader of such materials that he will surely go to hell if his ways are not mended.

It is common enough for persons to use special knowledge in gaining possession of items of which the true value is unknown to the owner. The record-breaking $2.5 million sale of "Icebergs" by American artist Frederick Edwin Church took place recently. The work, painted in 1861, and then acclaimed as "the most splendid work of art that yet has been produced in this country,"[13] was hanging in a school for boys, Rose Hill, which was originally the home of Sir Edward Willard Watkins, who had bought the painting around 1861. At his death in 1901, the house and its possessions went to the school. The fascinating part of this story is that before the sale, the school was "unaware of who had painted the work or what is was worth."[14] It actually hung unframed in a stairway for many years. A canny or unethical person could likely have had the painting at a low price and resold it at a handsome profit. Manchester Social Services, the firm that owned the painting, was apprised of its value by James P. Miller of Sotheby's who had recognized the painting from a photograph.

Dishonesty can take the form of withholding information, and it is hypothesized by Gerold Leone, a law librarian at New York University, in an article entitled "Malpractice by Law Librarian: Rhetorical Question—Or Is It?" in the *National Law Journal* of November 6, 1979, that suit could be brought against a library for such practices. No such case has yet come before the courts.

Leone, however, speculates upon this possibility. As access to information grows, he suggests, the closer the possibility comes: "What was once considered the hallowed preserve of a judge, practitioner, law student, and related government officials, more and more is becoming accessible to the lay public."[15]

Because this is so, Leone says, a person pursuing a *pro se* case (serving as his own attorney) can expect, and even demand, "whatever assistance may be required."[16]

A question arises as to whether or not the librarian must warn the patron of pitfalls that might be encountered in the case. Obviously, the more the librarian undertakes in such a matter, the greater is the risk he or she runs of being sued. Going afield for an example, Leone mentions a possible case in which a man comes to a reference librarian to build a patio and the patio, after the patron has followed the instructions in a book suggested by the librarian, falls. Questions a court might ask include: "Why did the patio fall?"; "What was the result of the failure (the falling patio)?"; and "Was insufficient information provided the patron, and if so did this result in damage?"[17]

Ohio College Library Center terminals have been in use since 1972. The first theft of such a terminal, valued at $3,700, took place in 1979 at the Library Department of the City College of New York.[18] Earlier thefts of OCLC terminals may have occurred, but this was the first reported in the library press. The story appeared in the *Library Journal* of June 1 of that year under the heading "Nail Down your OCLC Terminals."[19]

The advice proffered in this heading was good. In fact, libraries have for years been locking and bolting down ordinary office machines. The need to do the same with computers and their auxiliary equipment is apparent. The question of why anyone would steal a terminal might arise. Aside from resale, the terminal could be used by the thief in a computer operation of his or her own. Or, supposing the knowledge was available, it would be possible to tap into the OCLC system.

A more common kind of employee dishonesty is the misappropriating of the money from library fines. While the fines themselves are small, their total over a period of time can amount to a sizeable sum. One way of countering such dishonesty is for the library to use cash registers with a display which indicates to the patron how much money is being deposited. It is useful if the register has also a tape which monitors and records the amounts that are collected. Thus, someone who entered the figures would have to account for any monies missing. "No Sale" ring-ups are also counted, and suspicion would fall on areas where there are an odd number of such happenings.[20]

NOTES

1. Selwyn Rabb, "Library Ousts Store Manager After Paying $82,000 for Fake Supplies," *New York Times*, July 10, 1979, p. B3.

2. David J. Bauer, quoted in Rabb, "Library Ousts," p. B3.

3. Ibid.

4. Ibid.

5. Ibid.

6. Stanley Abrams, *A Polygraph Handbook for Attorneys*, p. xi.

7. John Marks, *The Search for the Manchurian Candidate*: The CIA and Mind Control, p. 22.

8. Anonymous interview.

9. "Rug Robbers?," *New York Times*, Sept. 2, 1979, p. 31.

10. "Ceremonial Collar is Missing at Yale," *New York Times*, Sept. 29, 1979, p. 24.

11. "The High Cost of Security," *Library Journal* 104 (May 1, 1979), p. 998.

12. Kenneth A. Briggs, "Scholars Search in Ethiopia in Study of Early Christians," *New York Times*, Aug. 12, 1979, p. 14L.

13. Rita Reif, "U.S. Painting Sold for Record $2.5 Million," *New York Times*, Oct. 26, 1979, p. 1.

14. Ibid.

15. Gerold Leone, "Malpractice by Law Librarians: Rhetorical Question—Or Is It?," *National Law Journal*, Nov. 5, 1979, p. 28.

16. Ibid.

17. Ibid.

18. "Nail Down Your OCLC Terminal," *Library Journal* 104 (June 1, 1979), p. 1207.

19. Ibid.

*It hath always been difficult so to limit men
by the laws of honesty that the knavery of
succeeding generations should not strive to
overleap the limits set by a preceding one
and break the established rules.*

Richard De Bury

LEGALIZED THEFT

There are methods by which unscrupulous persons may obtain library materials illegally and keep them without fear of prosecution. A despicable practice that has been noted is for an adult to have a child take out in his or her behalf materials which the adult has no intention of returning. Parents or guardians, at least in New York, cannot be held responsible for the material taken out by children:

> We thus conclude that in the absence of statute or the express assumption of legal responsibility by a parent or guardian for books borrowed by his child or ward, a public library has no civil recourse against such parent or guardian nor, for that matter, against the child, except perhaps to suspend his library privileges.[1]

Persons who admit that materials are lost and then pay for them gain a right to the materials. A case occurred at the Enoch Pratt Free Library in which a patron took out valuable children's books and reported them lost. The patron knew that under library regulations he would only be charged the printed price of the book, even though the books were valuable collectors items. The library erred in having such books on the shelves and in maintaining a policy which did not reflect the actual replacement cost of its lost books. New York law is such that technically this ploy is illegal, even though the payment has been made for the materials which are claimed to have been lost. Technically, one is still guilty in such an instance of violating the law, as it is a misdemeanor to keep property worth more than ten dollars which one has neither the authority nor right to possess or use.[2]

A much-used method of spiriting reference works out of libraries has been to paste false book pockets in the volumes so that to the unwary, the book seems to be one which is from a circulating collection. A way of preventing the loss of these works that has proven effective in major research collections is to require the checking at the door before admission to the premises of books from circulating collections or other libraries. Exceptions are generally allowed in the case of scholars who are doing research. It is true, of course, that the exceptions need vetting, but this presents no particular problem.

NOTES

1. Joseph Eisner, comp., *Handbook for Laws and Regulations Affecting Public Libraries in New York State*, p. 5-4.
2. Laurie Adams, *Art Cop: Robert Volpe-Art Crime Detective*, p. 43.

Twentieth century witchcraft.

Senator Sam Ervin

ELECTRONIC SECURITY

Electronic security systems are not the panacea that some have declared them to be. Technical and legal considerations complicate their use. It is these considerations that have prompted Alice Harrison Bahr to say in *Book Theft and Library Security Systems: 1978-1979*: "Studies indicate that electronic security systems can be effective book theft deterrents, but alternate theft prevention programs have also been successful."[1]

Electronic systems can, of course, be compromised by the thief or prankster who has a way with gadgets. And there are other problems. Once is the prevalence of false alarms that even the best system allows. Invariably, the arrangement is that the system reacts when an item with an unsuppressed signal is moved through a sensing device. Books are desensitized when they are checked out so they will pass through the sensing device without activating the alarm. Often enough, however, foreign metallic objects set off the alarm accidentally. Keys, belt buckles, pens, and the like can produce this effect. The result is embarrassment for all, if nothing worse.

Sensitizing large collections is a fairly expensive procedure. At least part of the expense may be avoided by sensitizing every fourth book or so, but whether or not this economy is worthwhile is debatable.

The advent of an electronic security system in 1966 at the Michigan State University Library was heralded by *The Dispatch* in an editorial of December 12, 1966 entitled "Electronic Library Guards" as a way in which privacy could be ensured at the checkout desk: "Not only is the new electronic system cheaper and more foolproof but it actually allows for more privacy in the often embarrassing and ticklish job of searching suspects."[2]

One aspect of the electronic security system librarians like is that it is impersonal. The Director of Libraries at Western Michigan University, Dr. Katherine Stokes, was quoted in *College Management*: "But, the best feature is that it is impersonal. You don't have to accuse a person of stealing a book. The machine does it. And we take the attitude that it's all a mistake."[3] Such an attitude is interesting. It indicates a disinterest or perhaps an aversion to matters of security—or at least an unwillingness to confront culprits with their deeds. The fact is, of course, that mistakes do happen, and it is better to acknowledge this than to involve the library in endless wrangles.

Matt Roberts expounds the conservative point of view in the matter of the efficacy of the electronic detection system: "It is unfortunate that electronic detection is not the answer to the theft problem. It is a reasonably good idea in theory; however, its cost makes it impractical, while its inherent weaknesses make it unworkable."[4]

A look at the cost factor is enlightening. Sensitizing a major collection, even if only every sixth or seventh volume is involved, can cost anywhere from twenty-five cents up per volume. This does not take into account the cost of special exit portals and the other related equipment.

Some systems do not operate on the magnetic principle. The manufacturers of one nonmagnetic system advertise that if their alarm goes off, it can only mean that there is a concealed book on its way out of the library. This is true. The system, which utilizes a laminate, is foolproof in this respect. Unfortunately, however, there are ways of smuggling a book through the exit without removing the laminate. It turns out that every system has its shortcomings and that none is really superior to any other.

Every system, be it electronic, magnetic, or microwave, can be beaten. One premise guiding the installation of an electronic detection system is that the presence of the system will deter the casual thief. And while this is likely so, the cost of the system must be balanced against deterrence and any other benefits that accrue.

Many instances are recorded in which the theft rate has been lowered. Equally frequent, unfortunately, are instances of costly breakdowns and maintenance failures; and there are those, too, in which it is apparent that the installation was unnecessary from the start.

A number of works have been published in recent years on

electronic detection systems. Among these is Alice Harrison Bahr's book, *Book Theft and Library Security Systems: 1978-1979*. This is a useful compendium on book theft and its prevention. Actually, it provides so much information that it could almost serve as a handbook on how to rob a library. Another useful work is Nancy H. Knight's "Theft Detection Systems—A Survey,"[5] which appears in the November 1976 issue of *Library Technology Reports*. This article deals with usage and operation of the six major systems (Book Mark, Checkpoint Mark II, Gaylord Magnavox, Knogo Mark II, Sentronic, and Tattle-Tape Spartan). The article includes a user survey and the materials provided by the manufacturers. Many books on security also provide additional information.

If it seems worthwhile to invest in a system, and this has been so in countless cases in recent years, cost is a secondary consideration in the matter. Even studies to determine the feasibility of a system can be expensive. Robert N. Sheridan reports as follows on the conducting of the inventory needed to pinpoint losses:

Average time per thousand for counting items in shelf list—42.4 minutes;

Average time per thousand for counting books on the shelf—34.1 mintues;

Average time per thousand for counting items in circulation (counting of individual charge records)—92.17 minutes.[6]

Patron acceptance of the machine is generally, but not always, good. Assuming that the machine is functioning well and that the library is relatively certain that an alarm has sounded erroneously, what should be done? Sheridan and Martin offer the following:

...the insistent denial of the patron and the sometimes angry and loud refusal to even return to the desk generally led the staff to open the gate and allow the patron to leave in order to avoid an unpleasant scene. It is however the staff's opinion that none of these patrons will try again to remove library material by carrying it through the sensing area.[7]

Sheridan and Martin suggest various ways of addressing the patron when the alarm goes off:

—Could you have accidentally jarred the clock as you walked by? That might have caused the alarm.

—Maybe the machine made a mistake. Would you walk through again just to see if it gives the same signal?

—Our book detection equipment seems to get the same signal from your book as from one of ours. Could I see it please?

—Your purse (package or brief case) may be alarming our system. May I take it through the gate to see if it caused the alarm?

—Did you forget to return the key to one of our restrooms? We have lost so many keys we have sensitized them, too.[8]

The decision had been made that to avoid involving Levittown in possible lawsuits, no one would be accused of book theft if they set off an alarm.[9] This was for obvious reasons a prudent course of action.

Another finding at Levittown was that the greater the sensitized portion of the collection, the lower the loss rate:

> Based on the evidence detailed above, there is a direct relationship between the degree of loss reduction achieved and the degree of sensitization. However, the extent of protection transfer from the protected to the unprotected portion of the collection shown should not be overlooked. It would appear that higher reduction in loss rates can be achieved in collections sensitized at a low density if the items to be sensitized are selected by the library staff rather than chosen at random. However, the additional cost involved in this procedure must not be overlooked.[10]

It is possible for lawsuits to be directed from another quarter. Some of the systems emit low-level EMR (electromagnetic radiation). While the magnitude of this radiation is low, it is high enough that sale of the machines is prohibited in Europe. There has been evidence, accepted in some quarters, that such emissions affect the nervous system and behavior. One can hardly believe that lawsuits are likely in the United States, but even the unlikely has an uncanny way of proving itself real.[11]

These devices seem to be meeting with library approval, and there has been little objection to them on the public's part. The devices clearly are here to stay.

Perhaps the most sensible attitude toward such devices was summed up by Louis J. Romeo in "Electronic Theft Detection

Systems, Part 1: Small College Libraries" in *Library and Archival Security*:

> No system is 100% effective. There will always be the student with a mind inventive enough to find a way of compromising the system. Librarians believe that electronic theft detection systems are an aid to the forgetful student and stop impulsive thefts. But as one librarian lamented: "I wish we could do better at the planned theft. But no system can protect against that sort of activity."[12]

Libraries have come a long way since the arrival of the 1964 Sentronic System of General Nucleonics.[13] And newer and better systems are constantly appearing.

NOTES

1. Alice Harrison Bahr, *Book Theft and Library Security Systems: 1978-1979*, p. 4.
2. "Electronic Library Guards," *The Dispatch*, Columbus, Ohio, Dec. 12, 1966, p. 1-B.
3. Dr. Katherine Stokes, quoted in "The Tell Tale Buzz," *College Management* 104 (Nov. 1966), p. 11.
4. Matt Roberts, "Guards, Turnstiles, Electronic Devices, and the Illusion of Security," *College and Research Libraries* 29 (July 1968), p. 272.
5. Nancy H. Knight, "Theft Detection Systems—A Survey," *Library Technology Reports* 12 (Nov. 1976), pp. 575-690.
6. Robert N. Sheridan, "Measuring Book Disappearance," *Library Journal* 99 (Sept. 1, 1974), p. 2041.
7. Robert N. Sheridan and Pleasant W. Martin, *Results of Tests Conducted to Determine the Need for a Book Theft Deterrent Device and the Ability of the 'Tattle-Tape' Electronic Book Detection System to Reduce Book Theft*, p. 18.
8. Ibid., Appendix III, pp. 2-3.
9. Ibid., p. 10.
10. Ibid., p. 16.
11. Bahr, *Book Theft*, p. 35.
12. Louis J. Romeo, "Electronic Theft Detection Systems, Part 1: Small College Libraries," *Library and Archival Security Journal*, 2:3/4 (Oct. 1979), p. 14.
13. Ibid., p. 1.

He who has vain fears deserves those that are real.

Seneca

THINGS THAT GO BUZZ IN THE NIGHT

The concept of an intrusion alarm hooked into a line which alerts the police is comforting in the abstract, but of dubious value in actual operation. The false alarm rate for units is such that in 1978, about 90 percent of all security calls received by local police departments were false alarms. John R. Holbrooks writes: "You may have the fanciest burglar alarm system on the market but to the police dispatcher it's just another light on a switchboard or a recorded message."[1]

The more sophisticated a system, the more prone it is to oversensitivity and consequently to false alarms: "Audio or vibration devices may not be able to tell the difference between a dropped crowbar and a sonic boom."[2] Ultrasonic systems can be compromised by thieves who move at a deliberately slow rate of motion and keep behind large objects such as crates or desks. Passive infrared alarms can be set off by heat from a duct or a shaft of sunlight coming into the protected area.[3]

A useful device that can be added to an intrusion alarm system is a microphone monitor. With this, the police can hear what is going on in the property.[4] Such devices, while costly, are effective in that the sounds of a burglary in progress bring an immediate response from the police.

NOTES

1. John R. Holbrooks, "Burglar Alarms: What's Reliable, At What Price?," *Inc.* 1:9 (Dec. 1979), p. 108.
2. Ibid.
3. Ibid.
4. Ibid.

117

Contributors for Insuring Houses, Chambers or Rooms
from Loss by Fire by Amicable Contribution Within
the Cities of London and Westminster and the Liberties
thereof and the Place thereunto Adjoining.

Name given first insurance company
organized, London, November 12, 1696

INSURANCE

Insurance is a necessary commodity to libraries and museums. This discussion ignores the insurance of general collections and buildings. Rather, it deals with the insuring of rare books and manuscripts.

The fine arts policy is an all-risk policy which is used for coverage of pictures, etchings, tapestries, rugs, statuary, and other valuables. The works covered, according to the carrier (insurance company), must be "bona fide works of art or rarity having historical value or artistic merit."[1] A complete listing of articles insured is a requirement of such a policy. Many institutions take photographs of their objects in addition to having written descriptions. Another useful, though expensive, recording technique is the videotaping of collections. This technique is usually employed in ongoing fashion to supplement or replace existing records. The fine arts policy covers damage or loss from fire, theft, and other hazards.

Most such policies have a requirement that could be burdensome—they require the listing of all of the items to be insured. However, there is a policy especially designed for rare books and manuscripts. This is the valuable papers and records policy. It has two sections: One section is for rarities which must be individually listed, and the other is a blank section which provides for lump-sum coverage of items which are not rarities. What is particularly attractive about this policy is that it provides "reimbursement, depending on the amount of insurance carried, for cost of research needed to reconstitute card catalogs, shelflists, payroll records, and any other library operating records." It may also cover the actual cost of replacing or reproducing the books lost.[2]

It is essential when buying insurance to obtain the best professional advice available. In this way, the library is assured that the complexities of its insurance problem are dealt with adequately. For example, it is necessary to know that the valuable papers and records policy does not provide for co-insurance. Co-insurance is an agreement under which insurance is maintained at a specific percentage of the value of the collection. The co-insurance policies are generally offered at a lower rate than that at which so-called flat insurance is available.[3]

The American Library Association, in cooperation with the Hartford Fire Insurance Company, has developed a special policy that is in use in forty-two states. This policy covers loss and damage contingencies, but not much more. Major collections generally need the further coverage provided by other policies.

The problems that insurance is designed to counteract are many and varied. One is damage caused by sprinklers that leak or go off when there is no fire. Most policies carry an exclusion for flood and water that backs up through sewers and drains.[4] Each policy is written separately and is therefore different in one or more respects from all other policies. Whether or not a company would pay for damage to water-soaked books and the expense of, say, centrifuging or freeze-drying them is a question that depends for an answer upon what is in the policy and its riders.

The thorny question of evaluating materials in a case of loss or of providing evidence of their value demands close attention. Paradoxically—if not too surprisingly—rare books and other items which are specifically covered for a given amount pose less of a problem than materials covered under the blank section of the policy. Nothing, however, is easy; and so having a good working relationship with one's broker gives one the comforting sense that even the most difficult problem will eventually, with the broker's help, be unravelled.

One of the more important sections of a policy is that containing the valuation clauses. They are generally of four types:

1. Valuation clause based on a schedule, either as part of the policy itself or on file with the insurance company. This type of clause allows for absolutely no value flexibility, and requires that the museum initiate any value change directly with the insurance

company. Only those works of art shown on the schedule are covered for insurance.

2. Valuation clause based on values contained in the registration or accession records of the museum. The wording of this clause elminates the necessity of supplying the insurance company with a long schedule and allows the museum to make value adjustments internally.

3. Valuation clause based on the actual cash value of the work of art at the time of loss. An excellent clause because it allows for market appreciation. However, there is a pitfall—such a clause allows for market depreciation as well.

4. Valuation clause based on the registration records of the museum or on the museum staff's estimate of value at the time of loss, whichever is greater. Obviously this is a very special clause, and is available only to institutions fully and professionally staffed, and willing to undertake an almost continuous appraisal and inventory of their numerous collections.[5]

Deductible losses are always a matter of concern. The larger the deductible, the less the insurance coverage. Deductibles vary in size but can range up to $5,000. Yet cases have been reported where the use of a $1,000 deductible has saved what amounted to two or three times that amount in premiums.[6]

Exhibits in glass cases and loan exhibits should also be covered. The insuring of loan exhibits is expensive, as such insurance must cover all contingencies from the time the exhibit leaves its home until it returns.

In investigating a library's insurance needs, a very good idea is to start by talking with the person in charge of security. This person will have some knowledge of insurance matters and can advise regarding firms with which the library might deal. Beyond this, the security person's input in the planning of coverage is bound to be useful.

As for the reviewing of a library's policies, this is a necessary procedure in a time of high inflation and should be seen to at least annually.

NOTES

1. Oscar M. Trelles, "Protection of Libraries," *Law Library Journal*, August 1973, p. 251.

2. Ibid.

3. American Library Association, "Insurance for Libraries Committee: Annual Report," *ALA Bulletin*, May 30, 1936, p. 383.

4. Trelles, p. 254.

5. Huntington T. Block, "Insurance: An Integral Part of Your Security Dollar." In *Protecting Works of Art*, Gerald Shirar, comp., p. 45.

6. Ibid.

*I only have one fantasy. We all start off naked
tomorrow morning—unsheltered, unfed,
unarmed—and see who survives.*

Robert Volpe

THE SURVIVOR

Robert Volpe is an artist and trouble-shooter who is also a
cop. Technically, Detective Robert Volpe is a member of the
New York Police Department's Special Investigation Division
assigned to the Art Recovery Team. Actually, Volpe is the one-
man force which has brought the art world to an understanding of
the need for action to combat the growing problem of art theft.
His colorful personality and the interest of his exploits have
always attracted press attention. Volpe reciprocates the warmth
the press has for him: "I love the press, which I have been criti-
cized for, but they have been as supportive as if they were my
family...They brought attention to a problem which I couldn't
have done alone."[1]
It was Volpe who called public attention to the pillaging of art
collections and the great increase in the incidence of art theft.
Before 1970 no one officially recognized that such a problem
existed. His expertise until recently was more appreciated and
admired in Europe, where art thefts are seen in a far more
realistic manner than in the United States. He is an intimate of
members of Scotland Yard and Interpol, and he has been the
subject of television specials in England and Germany. His importance as an authority on art theft is now fortunately recognized
everywhere. This is evidenced by the fact that he has also been
interviewed some 800 times in recent years in the United States.
One of the youngest men ever promoted to the rank of detective,
Robert Volpe began his career in the narcotics squad. He is a
practicing artist, and his interest in art theft appears to have
developed as a natural outgrowth of his talents as an artist.

Criticisms are leveled against every figure in the public eye. And Volpe is no exception. Some find his courting of the press distasteful. Others contend that his lack of academic credentials in art make his appraisals of art works suspect.

For all that, Volpe continues to do his work with remarkable success. It should be made clear, of course, that although he has no degree in art, he has taken numerous courses, both studio and classroom, in art. If Volpe is asked how many years of experience he has in art, he will say that he has been an artist for thirty-seven years, which is his age.

Volpe's appraisals of works of art are sometimes carried out in situations which are unorthodox and dangerous: "I recall one time I had to authenticate two stolen Remington bronzes in the back of a warehouse in dim light with a gun in my ribs."[2]

It is the creation of art which particularly interests him "An artist must create or die. That's why you don't see artists going on strike."[3] The idea of art being stolen is something which is of great concern to him. He equates the stealing of a piece of art with the theft of books: "If somebody went into our libraries and removed all the books, and one copy of those books is all that existed, they'd be lost forever."[4]

Volpe views art as a great national heritage. Unfortunately, Volpe explains this view is not shared by all: "You painstakingly go through burglary reports in which miscellaneous property is listed. You call up and ask them what's miscellaneous—Tiffany shades, oriental rugs"[5] Volpe is determined to remove art from the realm of the afterthought, from the miscellaneous. And the battle, he says, is far from won.

No officially produced computer list of art thefts exists yet. The FBI has talked about the possibility of compiling one, but so far such a list has not materialized. Volpe has, however, designed his own, which lists thefts since 1971. He makes no charge for listing a theft. Distribution of the list is controlled.

The fact that the average person's appreciation of art tends to be elementary makes the prosecution of art theft difficult, and the same is true in the case of thefts of rare books and manuscripts.

A letter of October 18, 1979, sent by Duke University's circulation head Albert A. Nelius to major military collections says in part: "Duke University has undergone a major theft of books in the subject areas of Civil War Campaigns, regimental histories, and personal narratives."[6] One might envision a few volumes having been taken. Such is not the case. The letter continues: "It will take some time to make an inventory, but it is estimated that the loss numbers at least 700 volumes."[7] The remainder of the letter gives a description of the markings on the stolen volumes:

> As marks of identification (which of course will have been removed), let me mention that each book was originally marked with a Dewey classification number (973.7---) on the lower part of the spine, or front cover in the case of small books. Virtually every one of these books would have borne a bookplate, pasted inside the front cover, with the inscription "George Washington Flowers Memorial Collection, Duke University Library." The call number would have been written by pencil on the page following the title page and book pocket would have been pasted inside the book cover.[8]

It is regrettable that a loss of this magnitude should receive little press attention. Occasionally, reports will appear, but such as do tend to be sensational. A case in point is a story printed in *Today* under the title "American Heritage Down the Drain." In this article, it is reported that 250,000 pieces of documents and letters of the Continental Congress are being neglected by the U.S. National Archives to the point that their safety is jeopardized.[9]

Sensational stories are better than none. It is only in publicizing the need for security that money is allocated for it. A crosswalk is not installed at an intersection until an accident confirms the need for it. And while this is a sad commentary on the political process, it indicates with fair accuracy what is required before a change can be made. Officials have been slow to acknowledge the need for strong security in libraries and archival institutions, but that slowness is gradually disappearing. Whereas once it took a major disaster to convince people to spend money on security, now security is a regularly budgeted item in many institutions of the sort.

Museums have been reporting thefts during the past few years, and this constitutes a breakthrough in the direction of greater security and in effecting recovery of the stolen items. The practice is being adopted gradually by the library and manuscript world but is not universally followed. Security chiefs without exception are in favor of having thefts reported. They are joined in this by museum curators and by archivists and librarians.

The situation at ALA underwent a change, however, with the formation of the Ad Hoc Committee on Security of the Rare Books and Manuscripts Section of ALA's Association of College and Research Libraries. Professor Terry Belanger, Assistant Dean of the School of Library Service of Columbia University, headed the Committee. The first meeting was held on January 20, 1980 at Chicago's Palmer House. The charge of the Committee was promulgated as follows:

1. To work towards the creation of standards for marking of books and manuscripts for those who wish to do so.
2. To explore the presently existing procedures for theft alert and recovery, and if deemed appropriate, to work towards the establishing of better procedures for these purposes.[10]

At the Committee meeting held on June 30, 1980 at the Barbizon Plaza in New York City, a realistic attitude was evidenced toward security, and an understanding was reached concerning the problems and prejudices which the Committee would have to overcome. The membership of the Committee is, in addition to Chairman Belanger, as follows: Thomas D. Burney, Library of Congress; Peter Hanff, Bancroft Library, University of California, Berkeley; Carolyn Harris, University of Texas, Austin; Paul S. Koda, University of North Carolina, Chapel Hill; Daniel Traister, New York Public Library, Research Libraries; David Zeidber, George Washington University, Washington, DC.[11]

One merely has to glance at the *New York Times* to comprehend fully Volpe's warning that the timely reporting of thefts is essential if recovery is to be made. The "disappearance" of more than 150 rare books and 200 plates from the Library of Harvard's Museum of Comparative Zoology rated in excess of seven column inches in the March 16, 1980 *New York Times*. The *Times* article mentioned that the list of missing books appeared in various issues of the "Antiquarian Bookseller" (November 1979 and the four following; March 3, 1980). The publication to which the *Times* was referring was, of course, the *AB Bookman's Weekly*. What apparently made the story of interest to the *Times* was the use of the magic initials "FBI" in the title—FBI Investigates Loss of Rare Books at Harvard." The *Times* wondered why it had taken until March 1980, since the "disappearance" (?) had been discovered in November 1979, for the FBI to be alerted. As the Associate General Counsel of Harvard, Edward W. Powers, explained: "Our feeling was that publishing the list first was a natural thing to do."[12] The FBI Special Agent in charge of the Boston office, James Dunn, refused to comment upon a *Boston Globe* report that one of the books had surfaced for sale at the auction house of Sotheby Parke-Bernet.

Perhaps the most telling facet of the story was buried. It could not be ascertained when the books had "disappeared" because, according to Powers, many were "used infrequently." The librarians of the Comparative Zoology Museum had called in the librarian from the Houghton Library of Harvard to assist them in determining the extent of their loss. The value of the missing items was not commented upon by Harvard or the FBI, although the *Times* quoted "a person familiar with the case" as having said that they "are worth something like $250,000."[13]

The business community has seen the value of library security. The Knogo Corporation, a maker of library security devices, appears in *INC.* magazine's "The INC. 100," a list of small companies which have at least quadrupled their sales in the past five years.[14] Business researchers predict that by 1990 the U.S. market for security systems will reach $23 billion. The market is thus expected to triple from its present position.[15]

NOTES

1. Robert Volpe, Interview, Oct. 12, 1979.
2. Ibid.
3. Ibid.
4. Ibid.
5. Ibid.
6. Albert A. Nelius, Duke University, Letter, Oct. 18, 1979.
7. Ibid.
8. Ibid.
9. "American Heritage Down the Drain," *Today*, April 24, 1979, p. A14.
10. Minutes of the Jan. 20, 1980 Meeting of the Ad Hoc Committee on Security RBMS, p. 1.
11. Jacob N. Chernofsky, "Editor's Corner: Library Thefts," *AB Bookman's Weekly* 65 (April 14, 1980), p. 2842.
12. "F.B.I. Investigates Loss of Rare Books at Harvard," *New York Times*, March 16, 1980, p. 24.

13. Ibid.

14. Bradford W. Ketcham, Jr., "The INC. 100," *INC.* Magazine, May 1980, pp. 55-56.

15. "Futures," *Findout* 7:2 (March-May 1980), p. 2.

We must depend upon and greatly appreciate
your willingness to turn information over
to us for publication.... Your report may lead
to a recovery; equally important, it may help deter
your colleagues from acquiring a stolen work.

Bonnie Burnham, Stolen Art Alert
January 1980

SECURITY AND THE MEDIA

Suddenly library security was being discovered by publications which had generally disregarded the topic. The January 15, 1980 *Library Journal* carried a lengthy article by Noel Savage entitled "News Report 1979." A section of the article, "Security in Libraries," quoted from the Carnegie Report and mentioned Berkeley's theft problem. Predictably, the article also dealt with protection of people in the library. The rationale for inclusion of such a section was dubious: "New crime statistics show an unexpected surge in violence of all kinds."[1] Had it not been for the rather sensational premise "violence of all kinds," one wonders whether the item would have appeared. Almost in a sensational vein, the page dealing with library security mentioned the stabbing in the main reading room at the New York Public Library.[2]

The segment dealing with library security was more a summary of short blurbs and throwaway items which appeared in the pages of *Library Journal*. Nothing new was really said. Yet it must be admitted that merely having the topic discussed is progress of a sort.

The *Times* gave more coverage in two months to library security than *Library Journal* gives in twelve. The problem with *Library Journal* is that the items of interest to those concerned with library security are merely one-inch reports. We have seen how the *Times* carried an article on electronic security devices in the

Summer of 1979. The Westchester section of the *Times* followed
suit on March 16, 1980, with an article entitled "Security Devices
Help Libraries Shelve Thefts," by Harriet Miller. The author, a
freelance writer, reported that many Westchester libraries had
installed electronic security devices. The article was given to
positive responses to the concept of electronic security devices. A
reference was made to the Plainview, Long Island Library. What
was most striking in the article was a quote by Wendy Bloom of
the Westchester Harrison Library: "Nobody checks briefcases
in this library. We feel a library should be a friendly place, not
an armed fortress."[3]

It had to come. Both special sections, the Long Island and the
Westchester, have dealt with library security. Thus it was that the
Special Education section of the April 20, 1980 *New York Times*
carried an article by Janet Blanksteen entitled "The College
Library: Den for Thieves?" Most startling was the following
paragraph:

> The problem is worse than it was 10 years ago, not neces-
> sarily because theft is on the rise—librarians do not know
> how many books are stolen each year—but because the
> cost of replacing and, whenever possible, mending books is
> higher than ever.[4]

Why this paragraph escaped the blue pencil of an editor is a
mystery. This was the only reference by the author to the fact
that "theft was not necessarily on the rise."[5] It was, to this reader,
as if Janet Blanksteen did not want to report on this subject and
felt that she had to assure the readers that theft was not necessarily on the rise. The paragraph following this amazing revelation
quoted Donald Engly, Associate Librarian at Yale; "It certainly
isn't getting less and is probably worsening."[6] The Director of
M.I.T. Libraries, Jay Lucker, stated, "The time is approaching
when we will have to put a security system in."[7] Despite the views
of these and other professionals, the article seemed to be an
almost manic apologia to assure the reader that it was due to rising
replacement cost, and not increased theft, that the problem was
worse. Predictably, the article ended with a positive quotation
regarding the overall situation. Princeton's Donald W. Koepp

was used to assure the reader that all was well. "Part of Princeton's tradition is open stacks and sometimes that means some old books are left open on the stacks for a student to use."[8]

What was fascinating was that in its original story on March 16, 1980 on the Harvard "disappearance," the *Times* had been careful to use the word "disappearance" rather than "theft," yet suddenly on April 20th, the Harvard situation was referred to in the following manner: "In February, for example, an estimated $250,000 worth of books and valuable plates were stolen from the Library of Harvard's museum of Comparative Zoology."[9]

Each *Times* article seems to end with an upbeat phrase to assure the reader that things are not as bad as they seem. Perhaps the most innocuous throwaway line is the one which ended Harriet Miller's piece, "The library of my childhood is changing. Despite this, the public library is still the tuition-free American university. It must remain open."[10] Not once did the Miller article mention closing libraries, save for that almost Kafkaesque last sentence. To be charitable, it must be admitted that the Miller article was in the Westchester section's version of the Op-Ed page.

Mutilation of books and paintings usually does not get reported in any but specialized publications, unless the work is of extraordinary value of a well-known work such as Rembrandt's "Night Watch." An item appeared in *AB Bookman's Weekly* of March 17, 1980, with the headline "Vandalism at NYHS." Eight historical portraits were reported to have been damaged by unknown vandals. It was noted that the mutilation was reported by "employees of the Society who have been on strike."[11] That was all that appeared, merely that short notice.

Again, the follow-up to this story was to be found in the pages of the *Times*. The material related to the mutilation was buried in an article by C. Gerald Fraser, "Historical Society Makes Wage Offer," which began with the following words: "The strike at the New York Historical Society reached its 134th day Wednesday."[12] The last paragraph of the story was concerned with the mutilation of the portraits:

> Mr. Kreisman [spokesman for the NYHS] also said that no new information was available on the vandalizing of eight paintings in one of the society's galleries at the end of Feb-

ruary or the beginning of last month. At that time, the police reported that the paintings may have been damaged by a cigarette or cigarette lighter.[13]

Were it not for the interest in the strike and the reporting of that event, this information regarding the vandalism, would never have reached the pages of the *Times* under the byline of a *Times* reporter.

Hidden away in the back pages of the *Times* there continues to be fascinating items of interest to those of us in the library and museum security field. For example, the August 28, 1980, *Times* reported that two sailors had stolen a collection of solid gold bear figurines from the carrier Coral Sea. The bears were valued at more than $300,000 and were recovered when the sailors were taken into custody. The reason that the bear figurines were aboard ship was that they had been given to the Navy by the City of San Francisco in 1889. The figures were placed on the carrier Coral Sea in 1967 when the carrier was adopted by the City of San Francisco as "its own."[14]

Three days later, the August 31, 1980 *Times* reported that a 9 by 7 inch Georges Rouault painting, valued at $25,000 and insured for $12,500, had been stolen from the Michigan State Art Center. The painting, entitled "The Tramp," had been removed from its frame with a razor blade. The comment of the gallery director Joseph Ishikawa bordered on the incredible; "You don't count on people carrying razor blades around."[15]

The September 7, 1980 *Times* told of two devices which could be used in the fighting of forgery. Neither device, although patents were granted, has as yet been marketed. What was of especial interest was that one of the devices patented by two IBM researchers was said to be able to measure acceleration and pressure as well as horizontal and vertical strokes.[16] Thus, handwriting samples could be compared with those on file in a computer.

If one knows where to look, one can find items that are of great interest. There are items which herald advances in security and detection techniques as well as those items such as the quote by the Michigan State Art Center Director which make one wonder whether they are some reporter's idea of a bad joke. Yet we must admit that such comments and utterances are no joke. These are the attitudes and beliefs against which we must all inveigh if security is to be more than a bothersome topic administrators relegate to hirelings.

NOTES

1. Noel Savage, "News Report 1979," *Library Journal* 105 (Jan. 15, 1980), p. 180.
2. Ibid.
3. Wendy Bloom, quoted in "Security Devices Help Libraries Shelve Thieves," by Harriet Miller, *New York Times*, March 16, 1980, p. 16WC.
4. Janet Blanksteen, "The College Library: Den for Thieves?," *New York Times*, April 20, 1980, p. 10, Educ.
5. Ibid.
6. Donald Engly, quoted in "The College Library," by Blanksteen.
7. Jay Lucker, quoted in "The College Library," by Blanksteen.
8. Donald W. Koepp, quoted in "The College Library," by Blanksteen.
9. Ibid.
10. Harriet Miller, "Security Devices," p. 16WC.
11. "Vandalism at NYHS," *AB Bookman's Weekly* 65 (March 17, 1980), p. 2056.
12. Gerald Fraser, "Historical Society Makes Wage Offer," *New York Times*, April 18, 1980, p. C26.
13. Ibid.
14. "2 Sailors Held in $300,000 Theft," *New York Times*, Aug. 28, 1980, p. B9.
15. Joseph Ishikawa, quoted in "$25,000 Rouault Painting Stolen from Michigan State Art Center," *New York Times*, Aug. 31, 1980, p. B1.
16. "Fighting Forgery," *New York Times*, Sept. 7, 1980, p. 49.

Of all sad words of tongue and pen the
saddest are "it might have been."

John Greenleaf Whittier

DOORS THAT SHOULD BE CLOSED

It may seem that by advocating security, security checks, and restricted access, the nature of library service is being altered. Fortunately, such is not the case. Access to some materials is as free as it has ever been; and if the egalitarian ideal that all should have access to any and all materials must be limited in some respects by practical considerations, there is nothing new in this.

Special collections of rare books and manuscripts are visited by scholars, researchers, and other interested parties who can pass the scrutiny of the staff. The question of closed stacks is one that arouses partisan views both pro and con; sometimes one view prevails, sometimes the other. There is, of course, good reason to suggest that access to special collections be restricted.

The thoughts of Joseph Green Cogswell as to why he was delighted that the Astor Library was a closed corporation are interesting: "It would have crazed me to have seen a crowd ranging lawlessly among the books and throwing everything into confusion."[1] Cogswell was intent upon the preservation of the collection and wanted to see that it was properly used. He realized that the Astor collection was a collection of a special nature: "In the first place it could never supply one out of a hundred of the demands in the case of a popular book; and in the next place it would be dispersed to the four winds in five years."[2] Cogswell's attitude seems stern in this day and age; but if there were concerns in the last century about the behavior of library patrons, there are as many now.

It is certainly a surprise for librarians in public libraries to find that they must spend considerable amounts of time and psychic energy in dealing with patrons who are disorderly. Frank

De Rosa believes that the main security problem in libraries, other than those given over wholly to research, is dealing with the disorderly patron. Ten years ago, the problem was book and materials theft.[3] At that time, had one suggested a policy similar to that of the 1894 policy of the Astor Library on evening hours, the suggestion would have been met with guffaws or resentment at such a snobbish attitude. The Astor staff had stated that if the library were open at night, it would be "filled with objectionable people who would come here simply to get warm."[4]

Circumstances do change with the times. In 1979, David Aikman of *Time* wrote of the New York Public Library: "Especially in winter, platoons of tramps drift in from the neighborhood to sleep at the table or mutter at readers."[5] Attitudes, too, change, but the process here takes longer.

The idea of the right of the public to free access to the library is admirable, but is obviously not without problems. A case can be made for placing restrictions on the use of public collections; and this is occasionally done, despite the fact that restrictions fly in the face of every public librarian's belief that access should be unimpeded. Occasional suggestions are made to the effect that posting a fee, as in the old subscription libraries, is an idea that ought to be revived. The ingrained opposition to constraints of this sort is such, however, that it is unlikely that they could succeed, even if they were instituted.

Collections of special material are closely guarded, as they should be. The perception that restrictions of usage or strict rules are upsetting to the scholarly community may be accurate. Yet such restrictions are unavoidable in a careless—and, some say, larcenous—age; and they are acceptable if for no other reason than that they ensure the availability of material that is wanted. As Robert Schnare of West Point observes; restrictions are a nuisance, but lost materials are worse. People bridle when restrictions are imposed, feeling that they impede one's work. In the end, however, the restrictions make sense to even their obdurate opponents.[6]

We live in a society where, if we allow it, banks will fingerprint us with dry ink and affix this fingerprint to the back of our checks. Our social security numbers are the basis of student I.D. numbers, and appear on credit rating reports, in violation of the 1937 Social Security Act. We are a society in which each onslaught against our right to privacy is tolerated. Such being the case, security measures in libraries are tolerated as minor inconveniences. And, indeed, because of the untrustworthiness of the few, the many must be inconvenienced.

Boutiques on Madison Avenue and other such shops once kept their doors open to all. Now, the doors are locked, and one must ring to gain admittance. Customers have not gone elsewhere but have come to understand that this is for their protection as well as that of the stores. The rash of armed robberies of art galleries is beginning to cause doors here to be locked as well. This is an unhappy but necessary trend, and it could portend what is ahead in some areas of the library and archival worlds.

It could once be argued that the restrictions imposed at the Astor and Lenox Libraries smacked of class and ethnic prejudice. Yet if that were ever true, clearly it no longer is. Today what restrictions there are have been prompted by two concerns: the preservation and safety of the collections. Both concerns are real; and if overzealousness is sometimes found in the security measures of libraries, this happened seldom enough. An article that appeared in *Life* in 1884 depicts students as hanging from the battlements of the Lenox, from which cannons sprouted. The article, which was in the form of a conversation, took aim at the policies of the Lenox, which were thought stern and rigid. Among these, according to the article, was the form of inquiry used to "ascertain if the applicant has any real necessity for consulting any particular book in the library," and the delving into the matter of the applicant's financial standing.[7]

Rules can be oppressive. However, the need for some of them was present in the last century. Its need is no less obvious now.

The library community must follow the lead of the art community in creating a strong security posture. The concept of service, while of overriding importance, must not be allowed to obscure the needs of security. Books and other materials are amenable to theft.

Sometimes thefts are carried out by persons of impeccable credentials. Recently, it was reported, Ronald V. Whittington, a special education counselor who possesses a doctorate, was arrested in Clovis, New Mexico for having stolen historical items valued in excess of $250,000. Among the items in his possession, for which he was being held in lieu of a $25,000 bond were:

—an anecdote in Lincoln's handwriting
—copies of the 1787 Federalist Papers
—a first printing of the Constitution
—a first edition of James Fenimore Cooper's *The Spy*
—two Presidential messages
—paintings
—jewelry
—firearms[8]

While most of the items belonged to public collections, some, it appeared, had been stolen from homes in Texas, homes in which the scholar was a guest.[9]

This incident gives some credence to the widely held notion that most thefts of library and archival materials are the work of highly educated professional people, as these people have access to and opportunity to make off with materials put at their disposal. This is not to say that many behave badly—the proportion is miniscule—yet the few who do steal account for a considerable portion of the losses that occur.

Losses, moreover, are taking place on a surprising scale. Evelyn Samuel says: "Uniformed guards, closed circuit television, electronic sensing devices have become the accepted norm in academic libraries. Their ubiquitous presence testifies to a widespread problem of sustained loss."[10]

Six persons knew the combination that opened the Military Treasures Room of the National Archives. On July 16, 1979, it was discovered that an 1861 letter from Lincoln to his Army Adjutant General had disappeared. The January 6, 1980 *New York Times* quoted Inspector General Curt Muhlenberg, who headed the investigation: "No suspects developed at all—we're not going to get anywhere. One of the difficulties was that nobody can pinpoint at what point in time that thing may have disappeared."[11]

Acting Archivist James O'Neill commented that there was little hope of tracing the material through a sale to a dealer: "Some of these autograph buffs are eccentric. They get their kicks out of possessing and admiring the signatures secretly."[12] The final paragraph of the *Times* article speaks volumes about the need for tightened security measures: "Access to the combination lock on the Military Treasures Room has been cut to three persons, and no one is permitted in the room alone now."[13]

The problem of library and archival theft exists. It cannot be wished away. It must be met head-on and dealt with in forthright fashion. Security must become as essential a priority to administrators as is the service ethic.

NOTES

1. Joseph Green Cogswell, quoted in *The New York Public Library*, Phyllis Dain, p. 29.
2. Ibid.
3. Frank De Rosa, Interview, Aug. 27, 1979.
4. Astor Library Staff, quoted in *The New York Public Library*, by Dain, p. 8.
5. David Aikman, "Reading Between the Lions," *Time*, Oct, 8, 1979, p. 20.
6. Robert Schnare, Interview, Nov. 2, 1979.
7. "Popular Science Catechism. Lesson XVI. The Lenox Library," *Life*, Jan. 17, 1884, reproduced in Dain's *The New York Public Library*, illustrations section, unpaged.
8. "Teaching Counselor Held in Historical Papers Theft," *New York Times*, Nov. 29, 1979, p. A22.
9. "Historical Items Recovered," *Today*, Nov. 29, 1979, p. A4.
10. Evelyn Samuel, "Protection of Library and Archival Materials: A Case Study—New York University's Institute of Fine Arts," *Library and Archival Security Newsletter* 2:3/4 (October 1979), p. 1.
11. Inspector General Curt Muhlenberg, quoted in "Archives Theft," Richard Haitch, *New York Times*, Jan. 6, 1980, p. 33.
12. James O'Neill, quoted in "Archives Theft," Richard Haitch, *New York Times*, Jan. 6, 1980, p. 33.
13. Richard Haitch, "Archives Theft," *New York Times*, Jan. 6, 1980, p. 33.

BIBLIOGRAPHY

"A Degas, Not Missed, Is Recovered by Museum." *New York Times*, September 20, 1972, p. 93.

"A New Kind of Inventory." *Library Journal* 42 (May 1917), pp. 369-371.

Abrams, Stanley A. *A Polygraph Handbook for Attorneys.* Lexington, MA: Lexington Books, 1977.

Ad Hoc Committee on Security, RBMS, Minutes of January 20, 1980 meeting.

Adams, Laurie. *Art Cop: Robert Volpe: Art Crime Detective.* New York: Dodd, Mead & Co., 1974.

Adams, Randolph G. "The Character and Extent of Fugitive Archival Materials." *American Archivist* 2 (April 1939), pp. 85-96.

Aikman, David. "Reading Between the Lions." *Time* 114:5 (October 8, 1979), 18-20.

"American Heritage Down the Drain." *Today*, April 24, 1979, p. A14.

American Library Association. Library Technology Project. *Protecting the Library and Its Resources: A Guide to Physical Protection and Insurance.* Chicago: American Library Association, 1963.

American Society for Industrial Security. *A Guide to Security Investigations.* Washington, DC: ASIS, 1977.

"Archival Security Surveys." *Archival Security Newsletter* 6 (July 1976), p. 12.

Ash, Lee, ed. *A Biographical Directory of Librarians in the United States and Canada.* Chicago: American Library Association, 1970.

"Astor Library Troubles." *New York Sun*, March 4, 1873, p. 7.

Bahr, Alice Harrison. *Book Theft and Library Security Systems: 1978-1979.* White Plains, NY: Knowledge Industry Publication, 1978.

Barrett, Laurence. "Library Scholar Steals 21 Priceless U.S. Mss." *New York Herald Tribune*, May 3, 1958, p. 3.

Bean, Ruth Anne. "Theft and Mutilation of Books, Magazines, and Newspapers." *Library Occurrent* 12 (January-March 1936), pp. 12-15.

"Beethoven 'Books' Are Lost in Berlin." *New York Times*, September 15, 1951, p. L7.

Berry, John N. "To Catch a Thief." *Library Journal* 90 (April 1, 1965), pp. 1617-1621.

Blackburn, Robert H. "Photocopying in a University Library." *Scholarly Publishing* 2:1 (October 1970), pp. 48-58.

Blanksteen, Janet. "The College Library: Den for Thieves?" *New York Times*, April 20, 1980, p. 10.

Block, Huntington T. "Insurance: An Integral Part of Your Security Dollar." In *Protecting Works of Art*, compiled by Gerald Shirar. Washington, DC: ASIS, 1978.

Bordin, Ruth B., and Warner, Robert M. *The Modern Manuscript Library.* New York: Scarecrow Press, 1966.

Briggs, Kenneth A. "Scholars Search in Ethiopia in Study of Early Christians." *New York Times*, August 12, 1979, p. 14L.

Brill, Steven. "Muscled by the F.B.I." *Esquire* 90:8 (October 10, 1978), 18-20.

Brooklyn Public Library Security Department Training Memo No. 1, March 21, 1979, 3 pages.

"Bulletin." *Art Theft Archives Newsletter*, Summer, 1979, p. 16.

"Burney, Charles." *Encyclopedia Britannica*. 11th ed. Vol. 4.

Burnham, Bonnie. *Art Theft: Its Scope, Its Impact, Its Control.* New York: International Federation For Art Research, 1978.

Burns Security Institute. *National Survey on Library Security*. Briarcliff Manor, NY: Burns Security Institute, 1973.

Callendar, Newgate. "Crime." *New York Times Book Review*, November 4, 1979, p. 24.

"Carnegie Study Finds Theft Rising in College Libraries." *Library Journal* 104 (June 1, 1979), p. 1206.

"Casinos' Microphones Ruled Illegal in Nevada," *New York Times*, December 24, 1980, p. B4.

Cave, Roderick. *Rare Book Librarianship*. London: Clive Bingley, 1976.

"Central Library for Presidential Records Suggested." *New York Times*, November 11, 1979, p. 50.

"Ceremonial Collar Missing at Yale." *New York Times*, September 29, 1979, p. 24.

"Charged in Library Thefts." *New York Daily News*, March 16, 1977, p. 3.

Chernofsky, Jacob N. "Editor's Corner: Library Thefts." *AB Bookman's Weekly* 65 (April 14, 1980), p. 2842.

Clark, Robert F., and Haydee, George. "Your Charging System: Is It Thief-proof?" *Library Journal* 91 (February 1, 1966), pp. 642-643.

Cole, Dorothy Ethlyn, ed. *Who's Who in Library Science: A Biographical Dictionary of Professional Librarians of the United States and Canada.* New York: Grolier Press, 1955.

Cox, Henry Bartholomew. "Caveat Emptor: The Ownership of Public Documents." *AB Bookman's Weekly* 62 (September 4, 1978), pp. 1243-1261.

Dain, Phyllis. *The New York Public Library: A History of Its Founding and Early Years*. New York: The New York Public Library, 1972.

De Bury, Richard. *The Philobiblon*. Berkeley, CA: University of California Press, 1948.

Donson, Theodore B. *Prints and the Print Market: A Handbook for Buyers, Collectors, and Connoisseurs*. New York: Thomas Y. Crowell, 1977.

"Drug Raid Nets Cache of Stolen Books." *AB Bookman's Weekly* 63 October 1, 1979), p. 2054.

Duckett, Kenneth W. *Modern Manuscripts: A Practical Manual for Their Management, Care, and Use*. Nashville, TN: American Association for State and Local History, 1975.

Eisner, Joseph. *Handbook of Laws and Regulations Affecting Public Libraries in New York State*. Long Island, NY: Nassau County Library Association, 1976.

"Electronic Library Guards." *The Dispatch* (Columbus, Ohio), December 12, 1966.

Elser, George C. "Exit Controls and the Statewide Card." *College and Research Library* 28 (May 1967), pp. 194-196.

"F.B.I. Investigates Loss of Rare Books at Harvard." *New York Times*, March 16, 1980, p. 24.

"Fighting Forgery." *New York Times*, September 7, 1980, p. 49.

Ford, Corey. *Donovan of O.S.S.* Boston: Little, Brown, 1980.

Fowler, Gene. "Stolen Art Owners Sought Here." *New York Times*, September 19, 1972, p. 55.

Fowler, Gene. "Lawyer Arrested in Theft of $10,000 in Art Prints." *New York Times*, September 7, 1972, pp. 45, 51.

Fraser, Gerald. "Historical Society Makes Wage Offer." *New York Times*, April 18, 1980, p. C26.

"Frequency of Inventory." *Library Journal* 52 (September 1, 1927), pp. 827-828.

Frisch, Howard. Letter to the Editor. *New York Times*, November 1, 1979, p. A22.

"Futures." *Findout*, March-May 1980, p. 2.

Glueck, Grace. "Lost Da Vinci Mural Believed Discovered." *New York Times*, November 2, 1979, p. 1.

Grossman, Albert J. "Television-Museum Watchdog." In *Protecting Works of Art*, compiled by Gerald Shirar. Washington, DC: ASIS, 1978.

Gupte, Pranay. "Artful Thieves." *New York Times Magazine*, July 22, 1979, pp. 58-62.

Haitch, Richard. "Archives Theft." *New York Times*, January 6, 1980, p. 33.

Hamilton, Charles. *Scribblers and Scoundrels*. New York: Paul S. Eriksson, 1968.

Hamilton, Charles. *The Book of Autographs*. New York: Simon & Schuster, 1978.

Hanley, Robert. "Libraries in U.S. Caught in Money Squeeze." *New York Times*, April 8, 1979, p. 20.

Harrison, Wilson R. "Dating Documents." *Criminal Law Review* 3 (June 1956), pp. 383-393.

Hill, Robert W. Letter to the Editor. *New York Times*, May 19, 1958, p. 22.

"Historical Items Recovered." *Today*, November 29, 1979, p. A4.

Honan, William H. "The Hidden Met." *New York Times Magazine*, July 1, 1979, pp. 13-41.

Honan, William H. "The Once and Future Met." *New York Times Magazine*, July 8, 1979, pp. 16-26.

Huxtable, Ada Louise. "The Museum Upstages the Library." *New York Times*, October 28, 1979, pp. 31D, 39D.

Institute for Business Planning. *Lawyer's Desk Book*. Englewood Cliffs, NJ: Institute for Business Planning, 1978.

"Inventory, Insurance and Accounting." *A Survey of Libraries in the United States*. Vol. 4, American Library Association. Chicago: American Library Association, 1927.

"Inventory: Report of the ALA Committee on Library Administration." *ALA Bulletin* 3 (1909), pp. 207-208.

"Iowa Throws Book at Thieves, Delinquent Patrons." *Library Journal* 104 (August 1979), p. 1510.

Jaeckel, Christopher C. "Stolen." *The Collector: A Magazine for Autograph and Historical Collectors* 864 (March 1979), pp. 1-4.

Kaiser, Robert Blair. "Kennedy Archivists Hope for Wide Appeal." *New York Times*, October 22, 1979.

Kaske, Neal K. *A Report on the Level and Rate of Book Theft from the Main Stacks of the Doe Library at the University of California, Berkeley*. Berkeley, CA: University Libraries, 1977.

Keally, Francis. Letter to the Editor. *New York Times*, May 10, 1958, p. 20.

Kelen, Emery. "Hats Off to Daring Thief of Herr Freud's Cap." *U.N. Observer and International Reporter* II:II (December 1979), p. 6.

Kemp, Edward C. *Manuscript Solicitation for Libraries, Special Collections, Museums, and Archives*. Littleton, CO: Libraries Unlimited, 1978.

Kent, Allen, Lancour, Harold, and Daily, Jay E., eds. *Encyclopedia of Library and Information Science*. New York: Marcel Dekker, Inc., 1976.

Ketcham, Bradford W., Jr. "The INC. 100." *INC. Magazine*, May 1980, pp. 55-56.

Knight, Nancy H. "Theft Detection Systems—A Survey." *Library Technology Reports* 12 (November 1976), pp. 575-690.

Land, Robert H. "Defense of Archives Against Human Foes." *American Archivist* 19 (April 1956), pp. 121-138.

Leone, Gerold. "Malpractice by Law Librarian: Rhetorical Question—Or Is It?" *National Law Journal*, November 5, 1979, p. 28.

Luongo Adjustment Co., advertisement. *New York Times*, December 2, 1979, p. D37.

Lydenberg, Harry Miller. *History of the New York Public Library: Astor, Lenox and Tilden Foundations*. Boston: Gregg Press, 1972.

Marks, John. *The Search for the Manchurian Candidate: The CIA and Mind Control*. New York: Times Books, 1979.

Mason, Philip P. "Archival Security: New Solutions to an Old Problem." *American Archivist* 38 (October 1975), pp. 477-492.

McGrath, Anne. "I.L.A.B. Fair—The Biggest Ever." *AB Bookman's Weekly* 66:19 (Nov. 10, 1980), pp. 3115-3139.

Mellow, James R. "Monet and Mayhem." *New York Times Book Review*, November 4, 1979, p. 15.

Metcalf, Keyes DeWitt. *Random Recollections of an Anachronism*. New York: Readex Books, 1980.

Middlemas, Keith. *The Double Market: Art Theft and Art Thieves*. Hampshire, England: Saxon House, 1975.

Miller, Harriet. "Security Devices Help Libraries Shelve Thieves." *New York Times*, March 16, 1980, p. 16WC.

"Minnesota's Carleton College Reports Rare Book Theft." *Library Journal* 104 (May 15, 1979), p. 1097.

"Missing Books Section." *AB Bookman's Weekly* 61 (July 11-18, 1977), p. 280.

Mitchell, Ellen. "Libraries Tighten Book Security." *New York Times*, July 22, 1979, p. L13.

Moat, Edward. *Memories of an Art Thief*. St. James, London: Arlington Books, 1976.

Moor, Paul. "The Great Mozart-Beethoven Caper." *Hi-Fi* 27:3, pp. 72-77.

Montgomery, Paul L. "$200,000 in Art Works Found in 2 Lockers at Grand Central." *New York Times*, September 18, 1972, p. 30.

Morris, John. *Managing the Library Fire Risk*. Berkeley, CA: Office of Risk Management of Safety of the University of California, 1979.

Murfin, Marjorie E., and Hendrick, Clyde. "Ripoffs Tell Their Story: Interviews with Mutilators in a University Library." *Journal of Academic Librarianship* 1:2, pp. 8-12.

"Nail Down Your OCLC Terminal." *Library Journal* 104 (June 1, 1979), p. 1207.

Nelius, Albert A. Duke University. Unpublished letter, October 18, 1979.

"New and Noteworthy." *New York Times Book Review*, October 14, 1979.

Niederhoffer, Arthur. *Behind the Shield: The Police in an Urban Society*. Garden City, NY: Anchor, 1969.

"Now It's A Wave of Thefts of Historic Documents." *U.S. News and World Report* LXXXIII:10 (September 5, 1977), pp. 51-52.

Olsen, Arthur J. "Bookseller is Accused of Looting Musical Treasures in Germany." *New York Times*, January 28, 1960, p. 11.

Oxford English Dictionary, The Compact Edition. Vol. II. New York: Oxford University Press, 1971.

Pegden, Norman. "A Comparison of National Laws Protection Cultural Property." In *Protecting Works of Art*, compiled by Gerald Shirar. Washington, DC: ASIS, 1978.

"Periodicals Hit List." *Library Journal* 104 (October 15, 1979), p. 2153.

Phalon, Richard. "The Game Where Nobody Loses But Everybody Loses." *Forbes Magazine*, April 16, 1979, p. 55.

Prasad, Badri. *Problems of Misplacement, Mutilation and Theft of Books in Libraries*. Delhi, India: B.P. Goswami, 1968.

Price, Cheryl A. "Document Examination in American Archives." *Special Libraries* 68:9, pp. 299-304.

Printemps, advertisement. *New York Times Book Review*, November 25, 1979, p. 90.

"Questions and Answers." *Library Technology Reports* 13 (March 1977), pp. 123-131.

Rabb, Selwyn. "Library Ousts Store Manager After Paying $82,000 for Fake Supplies." *New York Times*, July 10, 1979, p. B3.

Reed, John F. "Ethics." In *Autographs and Manuscripts: A Collector's Manual*, edited by Edmund Berkeley, Jr. New York: Charles Scribner's Sons, 1978.

Reif, Rita. "U.S. Painting Sold for Record $2.5 Million." *New York Times*, October 26, 1979, p. C22.

Reif, Rita. "Leonardo Notebook is Sold for $5 Million." *New York Times*, December 13, 1980, pp. 1, 25.

Registration form Society of American Archivists, Register of Lost or Stolen Archival Materials, p. 1.

Reneker, Maxine H. "Study of Book Theft in Academic Libraries." Unpublished Master's Thesis, University of Chicago, 1970.

Riley, William J. "Library Security and the Federal Bureau of Investigation." *College and Research Libraries* 38:2, pp. 104-108.

Roberts, Matt. "Guards, Turnstiles, Electronic Devices, and the Illusion of Security." *College and Research Libraries* 29 (July 1968), pp. 270-273.

Robinson, Donald Bruce. "A Survey of the Attitudes Toward and Utilization of Security Measures in Selected Academic Libraries." Unpublished Ph.D. Dissertation, Florida State University, 1976.

Romeo, Louis J. "Electronic Theft Detection Systems Part I: Small College Libraries." *Library and Archival Security Newsletter* 2:3/4 (October 1979), pp. 1, 7-18.

Roseberry, Cecil R. *A History of the New York State Public Library*. New York: State Education Department of New York, 1970.

Rosolato, Guy. "Psychoanalytic Notes on the Theft and Defacement of Works of Art." In *Protecting Works of Art*, compiled by Gerald Shirar. Washington, DC: ASIS, 1978.

"Rug Robbers?" *New York Times*, September 2, 1979, p. 31.

Saffady, William. "Evaluating Coin-operated Copying Equipment for Library Application." *Library Resources & Technical Services* 20:2 (Spring 1976), pp. 115-122.

Samuel, Evelyn. "Protection of Library and Archival Materials: A Case Study—New York University's Institute of Fine Arts." *Library and Archival Security Newsletter* 2:3/4 (October 1979), pp. 1-6.

Savage, Noel. "News Report 1979." *Library Journal* 105 (January 15, 1980), pp. 167-181.

Schellenberg, Theodore R. *The Management of Archives*. New York: Columbia University Press, 1965.

Schindler, Pat. "The Use of Security Guards in Libraries." *Library Security Newsletter*, Summer 1978, pp. 1-6.

Schreyer, Leslie J. "Legal Ramifications of Manuscript Collecting." In *Autographs and Manuscripts: A Collector's Manual*, edited by Edmund Berkeley, Jr. New York: Charles Scribner's Sons, 1978, pp. 17-177.

"Security Shortcomings Assailed." *Library Journal* 104 (April 15, 1979), p. 878.

Sheridan, Robert N. "Measuring Book Disappearance." *Library Journal* 99 (September 1, 1974), pp. 2040-2043.

Sheridan, Robert N. and Martin, Pleasent W. *Results of Tests Conducted to Determine the Need for a Book Theft Deterrent Device and the Ability of the Tattle-Tape Electronic Book Detection to Reduce Book Theft*. Levittown, NY: Council on Library Resources, 1972.

Society of American Archivists. *National Register of Lost or Stolen Archival Materials: List A 1975-Present*.

"Society of American Archivists Security Consultant Service." Information package.

Sportouch, Georges. "Museum Attendants." In *Protecting Works of Art*, compiled by Gerald Shirar. Washington, DC: ASIS, 1978.

"2 Sailors Held in $300,000 Theft." *New York Times*, August 28, 1980, p. B9.

"$25,000 Rouault Painting Stolen from Michigan State Art Center." *New York Times*, August 31, 1980.

"Teaching Counselor Held in Historical Papers Theft." *New York Times*. November 29, 1979, p. A22.

"The High Cost of Security." *Library Journal* 104 (May 1, 1979), p. 998.

"The Melville Heist." *Library Journal* 104 (May 1, 1979), p. 994.

"The Tell Tale Buzz." *College Management*, November 1966, p. 11.

"Theft Guidelines Now A.B.A.A. Policy." *AB Bookman's Weekly* 63 (October 8, 1979), p. 2252.

Thomas, Robert McG., Jr. "Theft of Historic Letters from New York Library Laid to Autograph Dealer." *New York Times*, March 15, 1977.

Thompson, Lawrence R. *Robert Frost: The Early Years 1874-1915*. New York: Holt, Rinehart, and Winston, 1966.

Thompson, Lawrence R. *Robert Frost: The Years of Triumph 1915-1938*. New York: Holt, Rinehart, and Winston, 1970.

Thompson, Lawrence C. "Mutilantis Mutilandis." *Library Security Newsletter* 2:2 (Summer 1978), pp. 15-16.

Thompson, Lawrence C. "New Reflections on Bibliokleptomania." *Library Security Newsletter* 1:1 (January 1975), pp. 8-9.

Thompson, Lawrence C. "Notes on Bibliokleptomania." *New York Public Library Bulletin* 48 (September 1944), pp. 723-760.

Thompson, Lawrence C. "The Biblioklept Curses." *Library Security Newsletter* 1:6 (Nov./Dec. 1975), pp. 1, 8-9.

Tiranno, Natalie, and Chernin, Milton. "Rare Letters Stolen." *New York Mirror*, May 3, 1958, p. 3.

Tiranno, Natalie, and Chernin, Milton. "Rare Notes are Stolen." *New York Daily News*, May 3, 1978, p. 3.

Trelles, Oscar M. "Protection of Libraries." *Law Library Journal* 98 (August 1973), pp. 241-258.

"Vandalism at NYHS." *AB Bookman's Weekly* 65 (March 17, 1980), p. 2056.

Vinnes, Norman. "Search for Meaning in Book Thefts." *School Library* 18 (Spring 1969), pp. 25-27.

Walker, Ralph S. "Charles Burney's Theft of Books at Cambridge." *Transaction of the Cambridge Bibliographical Society* 3:4 (1962), pp. 313-326.

Walsh, Robert R. "Rare Book Theft and Security System Confidentiality." *Library and Archival Security Newsletter* 2:3/4 (1978), pp. 24-25.

Warren, Robert Penn. In "Legal Ramifications of Manuscript Collecting," by Leslie J. Schreyer. In *Autographs and Manuscripts: A Collector's Manual*, edited by Edmund Berkeley, Jr. New York: Charles Scribner's Sons, 1978.

Wayhrauch, Ernest E., and Thurman, Mary. "Turnstiles, Checkers and Library Security." *Southeastern Librarian* 18 (Summer 1968), pp. 111-116.

Williams, Sam P., Jackson, William Vernon, et al., compilers. *Guide to the Research Collections of the New York Public Library*. Chicago: American Library Association, 1975.

Wyden, Peter. *Bay of Pigs: The Untold Story*. New York: Simon and Schuster, 1979.

"Yale Security Eyed." *Library Journal* 104 (March 15, 1979), p. 665.

INTERVIEWS

Anonymous Interviews.

Burnham, Bonnie. Executive Director, International Foundation for Art Research. Interview, August 28, 1979.

Cohen, William. Director of Library Services, Haworth Press. Telephone Interview, May 7, 1979.

Cohen, William. Personal Interview, November 30, 1979.

De Rosa, Frank. Head of Security BPL. Interview, August 27, 1979.

Goodsen, Linda. American Society for Industrial Security. Telephone Interview, May 7, 1979.

Hammer, Donald P. Executive Director, ALA, LAMA. Telephone Interview, May 7, 1979.

Koslow, Donald. Assistant Director of Libraries, West Point. Interview, November 2, 1979.

McShane, Tom. FBI Agent. Telephone Interview, May 7, 1979.

McTigue, Bernard. Librarian, Arents Tobacco Collection. Interview, November, 14, 1980.

Metcalf, Keyes DeWitt. Telephone Interview, December 16, 1980.

Moss, Mike. West Point Museum Security. Interview, November 2, 1979.

Richter, Anne. Assistant Editor, *Library Journal*. Telephone Interview, October 4, 1979.

Rugen, Paul. Keeper of Manuscripts NYPL. Interview, October 5, 1979.

Schnare, Robert. Special Collections Librarian, U.S. Military Academy, West Point. Interview, November 2, 1979.

Szladits, Lola L. Curator, Berg Collection. Interview, December 15, 1980.

Volpato, Joseph R. Associate Manager Security, Metropolitan Museum of Art. Interview, August 16, 1979.

Volpe, Robert. Detective, NYC Police Force. Interview, October 12, 1979.

Walch, Timothy. Society of American Archivists. Telephone Interview, May 9, 1979.

Weiss, Egon A. Director of Libraries, U.S. Military Academy, West Point. Interview, November 2, 1979.